Praise for Bill Shore's *The Cathedral Within*

"Simply revolutionary."
—MARY MCNAMARA, *Los Angeles Times*

"Charming and effective . . . essential reading for business leaders."
—*Publishers Weekly*

"Positively invigorating."
—*Kirkus Reviews*

"*The Cathedral Within* is a reminder that what really counts in our lives and in our communities is the enduring values of giving back and helping others. Bill Shore is a true American visionary, whose written prescription of how we can all give something back is both inspiring and enlightening. This book can change both human lives and organizational lives for the better."
—SECRETARY OF STATE COLIN L. POWELL

"*The Cathedral Within* is a clarion call in this time of compassion fatigue, a compelling and convincing plea for us to reconsider the way we approach problems of hunger and poverty."
—RICHARD RUSSO, author of *Straight Man*

"Bill Shore is a master at inspiring, mobilizing, and leading people and companies to discover and act on their values in innovative new ways. His wisdom and insights into the transforming power of social purpose in our businesses and our lives provide essential reading for leaders everywhere."
—ROSABETH MOSS KANTER, Harvard Business School, author of *World Class* and *Rosabeth Moss Kanter on the Frontiers of Management*

"Bill Shore has done the impossible: written a social policy book that is a page-turner. Peppered with stories whose wit and wisdom delight us as they inform and inspire us, *The Cathedral Within* celebrates the human spirit. This book is mandatory reading for all who struggle against the odds to fashion a better future for all of America's children."
—LISBETH SHORR, author of *Common Purpose*

Also by Bill Shore

Revolution of the Heart

The Light of Conscience

The Cathedral
Within

The Cathedral Within

Transforming Your Life
by Giving Something Back

Bill Shore

RANDOM HOUSE TRADE PAPERBACKS

NEW YORK

Copyright © 1999, 2001 by Bill Shore

All rights reserved under International and Pan-American Copyright Conventions.
Published in the United States by Random House Trade Paperbacks, an
imprint of The Random House Publishing Group, a division of
Random House, Inc., New York, and simultaneously in
Canada by Random House of Canada Limited, Toronto.

RANDOM HOUSE TRADE PAPERBACKS and colophon are trademarks of
Random House, Inc.

This work was originally published in hardcover and in slightly different form by
Random House, an imprint of The Random House Publishing Group, a division of
Random House, Inc., in 1999.

Grateful acknowledgment is made to the following for permission to reprint
previously published material:
The New York Times: Excerpt from "Food's Ambassador to Washington," by
Marian Burros (The New York Times, September 30, 1998). Copyright © 1998
by The New York Times Company. Reprinted by permission.
Writers House LLC: Excerpts from Unfulfilled Dreams, by Martin Luther King, Jr.
Copyright © 1968 by Martin Luther King, Jr., and copyright renewed 1996 by
Coretta Scott King. Reprinted by arrangement with the Estate of Martin Luther
King, Jr., c/o Writers House as agent for the proprietor.

Library of Congress Cataloging-in-Publication Data

Shore, William H.
The cathedral within : transforming your life by giving something back/
Bill Shore.
p.   cm.
ISBN 0-375-75829-1
1. Philanthropists—United States—Biography.   2. Volunteer workers
in social service—United States—Biography.   3. Women in charitable
work—United States—Biography.   4. Children—Care—United States.
5. Charity organization—United States.   I. Title.
HV27.S535   2001
362.7'092'273—dc21
[B]   2001031774

Random House website address: www.atrandom.com

Printed in the United States of America

4   6   8   9   7   5

Book design by Mercedes Everett

For Zach and Mollie

Contents

1. Finding the Cathedral Within • 3

2. Starting Points • 31

3. Coming Up Taller • 79

4. The Battle Between Idealism and Cynicism • 99

5. A Pioneer of Community Wealth • 124

6. "We Are Now Challenged to Be
    Institution Builders" • 155

7. Lessons of a Storyteller • 187

8. You're Worth More Than You Think You Are • 202

9. Passion Rules the Universe • 233

10. When a Rock Pile Ceases to Be a Rock Pile • 260

Afterword • 270
Resource Directory • 280
Acknowledgments • 306

The Cathedral
Within

CHAPTER ONE

Finding
the Cathedral Within

I

I recently received a handwritten letter from a friend who left his job. He wrote, "What I want to do next, in addition to making some dough, is something that counts."

He is forty-three years old, has three young sons, and lives in the Washington suburb of Silver Spring, Maryland, where I also live. We've known each other more than a decade, having crossed paths in various political campaigns. He's been a small but steady contributor to Share Our Strength (SOS), the antihunger and antipoverty organization I founded, his check always accompanied by a heartfelt note complimentary of our work. His current stationery is distinctive, and when I saw his letter on top of a tall stack of mail on my desk, I wasn't sure what to expect. (Actually I don't have a desk. I sit at the same folding table I've used since SOS began fifteen years ago. There's more room for my legs and I'm too sentimental or superstitious to give it up. Besides, along with the rest of the nonmatching furniture that's been donated to our office, it reassures donors that we're spending their money the right way.)

"Something that counts." It's a revealing phrase. It holds the promise of both higher purpose and lasting result. There's an earnestness in its simplicity and plainspokenness. It's especially revealing when it's got the gold seal of the president of the United States embossed above it.

My friend's name is Mike McCurry. For three years he served as Bill Clinton's press secretary and managed to satisfy both the president of the United States and the press corps covering him. He left to a chorus of favorable reviews, culminating in NBC anchorman Tom Brokaw ending a nightly newscast with an affectionate "Good job, Mike."

I'm intrigued that Mike didn't say he wants to "continue" doing something that counts, but rather that it's what he wants to do "next." Mornings in the Oval Office, afternoons on Air Force One, and evening appearances on every television screen in the country would qualify, for some people. The White House is where the action is, the center of our national attention. Events in far corners of the world are influenced by what does or does not happen there. If working in the West Wing at a senior level doesn't count, then what does?

Don't get me wrong. I think McCurry loved being presidential press secretary. This was a job he not only coveted, but methodically groomed and prepared himself for over many years, and one at which he excelled. Starting with

John Glenn's presidential campaign in 1984, then Bruce Babbitt's in 1988, and finally Senator Bob Kerrey's in 1992, McCurry both learned the ropes and paid his dues. He managed to emerge from each loss with his good humor intact and his reputation enhanced. Ultimately, he accepted the post of spokesman for Secretary of State Warren Christopher, mastering the details and nuances of foreign policy and confidently handling the press corps. The State Department was a staging ground to catch the attention of the president, whose 1992 campaign he had opposed. When Clinton's first press secretary, Dee Dee Myers, left the White House, McCurry was brought in.

McCurry managed to weather the Clinton scandals and maintain not only numerous friendships in the press corps but, more important, his integrity. By the time he left, he was a well-known and well-liked TV personality. There were invitations to give speeches, write books, and lobby, as well as many other lucrative opportunities. As anyone in his position would, he took some of them. He's savvy enough to have no illusions about either his celebrity or the value he can derive from it in a celebrity-conscious marketplace. When he talks about doing "something that counts," he's not referring to society's definition. He means something that counts to him.

Doing something that counts. Something that not only makes a difference, but has a lasting impact. It's a basic human need, like water or calcium. We can actually get by with surprisingly little of either, but we hold together better and longer when we get regular servings of each. Wait, I'll go further; there's a better analogy. We need it like we need love. It's the need we aren't sure how to talk about, the one that makes us feel . . . whole.

This goes to the very heart of what Share Our Strength means and does. Everyone has a strength to share. Often it is a skill or talent they've come to take for granted, but one that can make a difference in the life of somebody else if properly deployed. Mentors share strength. So do tutors, coaches, and doctors. Chefs who teach nutrition to low-income families are sharing strength, as are college students who read to children in preschool Head Start programs. Sharing strength is as valuable as donating money. Sometimes it's worth more, because it cannot be bought.

All of us have strengths we need to share. The challenge lies in creating vehicles that enable diverse individuals to do so, especially that vast majority who may not think of themselves as community activists, civic leaders, or social entrepreneurs, or as part of a broader national service movement. It's not just about volunteering or trying to be a better person. It's not about making your community a better place. It's not about service being good for your soul. It is more fundamental, almost primal. It is what the species instinctively wants to do: to perpetuate itself by leaving something behind; to make a mark that lasts; to make ourselves count.

Each day the mail at SOS brings pleas for money, but

each day also brings pleas for meaning. I get a lot of letters like Mike McCurry's from college students and corporate executives, from mothers whose children are grown, and from businesspeople who have enjoyed prosperity but not necessarily purpose. They say they want to "give something back," to find a way to contribute that will be meaningful and make a difference. What they want to know is *how*.

There have always been such people among us: generous, altruistic, even idealistic. In recent years, their numbers have grown, but so have the opportunities to serve. Right now, the potential to bring about lasting change is greater than ever before, and so is the need. Today, there is another generation of Americans that desperately needs help: the generation of children who are poor, vulnerable, and destined to repeat a familiar cycle of dysfunction and despair that is incongruous and unnecessary in a prosperous America.

Historically, when faced with crisis, our society and government have responded—however untimely, slowly, or inadequately—with assistance that has been in direct, not inverse proportion to the nature of the needs at hand. This is no longer the case regarding the needs of children. At a point in modern American history when children are at their greatest peril—from violence, drugs, the breakdown of family, and social and economic trends trapping them in poverty—protections are being dismantled at every level. It is as if the mighty Mississippi River were flooding at record levels, and instead of piling sandbags high, the people and their government started carting them away, frustrated and angry that the river hadn't learned its lesson after all these years and chances.

That said, the sandbags we've piled up, some from as long ago as Franklin Roosevelt's New Deal, are not, by themselves, enough. Something is missing from the mixture of public policy and social science we've relied upon to produce healthy children. Of twelve million children under the age of three in the United States today, staggering numbers live in conditions that threaten their lives. One in four lives in poverty. We've been able to relieve misery, often just temporarily, but not to reverse it. This has been the case whether the prevailing winds were liberal or conservative.

In the midst of unprecedented affluence, America leads the industrialized nations in the percentage of children raised in poverty. The consequences for poor children are dire. They are more likely to have poor health, die during childhood, score low on standardized tests, have out-of-wedlock births, and experience violent crime. Such consequences are also preventable, as are the conditions that create them, but only if we approach them dramatically differently than we have in the past.

The social paradox of our time is that prosperity hides poverty. Good times distract us from the bad. When pain is not shared, it is not top-of-mind. Prosperity creates comfort, and comfort is the enemy of change.

By itself, even a massive new wave of talent serving in ways that are better and more effective may not be enough to save these kids, but it is one indispensable ingredient without which they have no chance at all. You may wonder if it is guaranteed that committing yourself to the task will change our country and their lives. It is not, but it is guaranteed to change yours.

Over the past four years I've traveled the country almost nonstop. From Boston to Battle Creek, from Arkansas to Arizona, from West Virginia to Wisconsin, I've met teachers, doctors, chefs, bus drivers, shoe salesmen, cookware manufacturers, artists, social workers, retailers, librarians, coaches, bankers, and thousands of others working to improve their communities. They shared ideas, best practices, and their experiences doing something that counts. The organizations they've built and the programs they run are fascinating, but what has stayed with me more vividly than what they said is what they showed of themselves and confirmed about human nature: that it embodies an irrepressible and infinite ability to create, express, give, and share strength. Those who do so grow stronger still.

Explorers are partial to bold declarations. When asked once how he would have designed the universe differently, Maarten Schmidt, a world-renowned astronomer at Cal Tech and discoverer of galaxies, exclaimed, "God! What a wild question. Sometimes it strikes me that the universe is much smaller than . . ." He hesitated a moment. "All right, here we go. I would have constructed a bigger universe. I think the universe is small. If I'd had my rathers, I would do that. I find the universe too confined. I find it amazing that it is so small."

This is a book about constructing a bigger universe, about the new ideas and new leadership of extraordinary people who are expanding the range of what is possible in communities across America and making the future larger for ourselves and for our children.

It is not my goal to write a book calling for new programs. Congress, state legislatures, and national and community foundations have already created thousands of them ranging from Head Start and school breakfasts to drug counseling and student aid. They serve vital purposes, but by themselves they are not enough. Nor is my objective to produce a book about finding new financial resources or the political will to create them, although that too is necessary.

My ambition instead is to design a new architecture for how society uses resources to help children, much like the cathedral builders of an earlier time, who combined imagination, invention, and faith to build something both magnificent and lasting. The great cathedrals did not grow skyward because their builders discovered new materials or suddenly found the necessary financial resources. Rather, they had a unique understanding of the human spirit that enabled them to use those materials in an entirely new way.

Prior to selling this book to a publisher nearly two years ago, I followed standard operating procedure and submitted a ten-page proposal. The working title (since abandoned) was "Cathedral of American Childhood." My agent, Flip Brophy, arranged for a meeting with an interested publisher, which turned out also to be the largest in the country, Random House. An editor there named Jon Karp, whom I'd met years earlier when he'd edited a book for my former employer, Senator Gary Hart, was leaning toward buying it. We scheduled an appointment, and the following week I was on the Metroliner to New York.

Karp wanted me to meet his boss, Ann Godoff, and invited her to join us. Both were in publishing because they believed in the power of ideas. They had a track record of publishing and marketing serious books. Flip considered it a real coup that both had taken an interest in my proposal.

Publishers sometimes acquire a book if they like the written proposal; often they buy a book because they believe it will have a large commercial audience and make money, and sometimes they will take a chance on a still developing proposal if they like the author. Both Karp and Godoff explained that my proposal, built around the metaphor of cathedral building, "was not quite there yet." Still, they seemed genuinely interested in my ideas and confident we could work something out.

Ann Godoff described the book she'd like to see written, the book she said she'd want to read. She went into what I could only describe as a literary jazz riff for about twenty minutes. Her tempo increased as she spoke, and I could feel myself not keeping up with her, like a runner falling behind at the turn. She concluded by saying, "So if that's what you want to write, if you want to write a book about the cathedral within, then that's a book I want to buy."

I looked over at Flip for reassurance and to see if she had been taking notes. I didn't understand more than a sentence or two of the entire twenty minutes. I hoped this wouldn't disqualify me from being a Random House author. I knew what a powerful platform a well-published book created for disseminating ideas and, more important, how much would become revealed to me in the writing and how much I'd learn.

After that initial meeting, I kept hearing the words "the cathedral within" in my mind. In fact, that was the only part of the editorial riff I could remember. "The cathedral within . . . the cathedral within." But over the course of the next two years, I began to understand Ann Godoff's insight. In searching for meaning in the precious economy of those three words—the cathedral within—I found a path more rewarding than any I've known, and perhaps the key to making America the country it can be. The universe I'd been contemplating was far too small. I came to see that the ambitious cathedrals I aspired to build were dwarfed by what could take shape instead within a person's heart and soul.

II

The cathedral of Milan is the second largest Gothic cathedral in the world. After more than five hundred years of construction, from 1386 to 1887, the interior is as spare and simple as the façade is crowded and ornate. As I stand inside it at sunset, the near-empty space gradually grows darker. For each of us traveling alone, the solitude draws closer, like an overcoat being fastened one button at a time.

The cathedral is built upon the ruins of the original fourth-century cathedral. Crystalline pinkish-white marble from the quarry at Candoglia was carried down a mountainside and loaded onto barges and then carried to Milan by waterways. Napoleon stood on it when he was crowned king of Italy here in 1805.

A few people pray in the quiet coolness and take confession. Others light candles. A circle of Asian tourists moves like a choreographed troupe. Schoolgirls in the last pew are sketching for art class. In the nave, several pairs of lovers take refuge. They whisper in voices only pillows have heard, relieved and grateful that the vast cathedral not only condones but demands intimacy. They are surrounded by stained glass so precious it was removed and hidden during World War II's bombing raids, the vivid colors unlike anything ever seen on canvas or screen.

All day long, Milanese on their way to or from work or market pour in for prayer or reflection. I step outside and watch them stream across the Piazza del Duomo from side streets and subway stations. Many are regulars, so accustomed to the towering spires outside and the brilliant stained glass within that they no more look up than New Yorkers do walking by the Empire State Building. When I step back inside, the cathedral is still empty; so vast is this space that one hundred people fill it no more successfully than do five.

Of at least one thing I'm certain: The builders of this cathedral did not consider inspiration and faith as by-products or fringe benefits of their work. Rather, it was the core purpose, the essential, uncompromisable ingredient of the entire architecture and design. Every other consideration was secondary to this. One can't stand in the aisles, dwarfed by the thirty-six massive pillars, staring at the unfathomable vaults and buttresses, and not know this to be true.

A cathedral of this magnificence cannot be built without people believing in it so deeply and so truly that their belief becomes contagious. It had to have taken more than salesmanship and communications skills to convince citizens across five centuries to bring the vision of this cathedral to fruition. There had to have been an authenticity that resonated in the hearts of others.

The vast majority of those who worked on this (and every other) cathedral did so knowing they would not live to see the final, finished achievement. This didn't diminish their dedication or craftsmanship. The evidence suggests it enhanced it.

Cathedral building required sharing strength on a scale never seen before or perhaps since. When construction commenced on the Milan cathedral, craftsmen came from across Europe—stonecutters, sculptors, master masons, blacksmiths, and carpenters—and cooperated to an unprecedented degree. While nobles made large financial donations, contributions came from all citizens, sharing whatever their strengths happened to be. Weavers, bakers, butchers, tanners, millers, and fishermen took turns donating their services, without salary, as did physicians and apothecaries. It is said the vicar worked in the stone yard. Groups of young women dressed in white went through town and countryside collecting offerings.

Somehow, it had been both communicated and understood that it wasn't just that building a truly great cathedral would require everyone to share their strength, but rather that everyone sharing their strength would result in a truly great cathedral.

The works of the cathedral builders endure to this day. In a world of ever more constant change, their achievements stand out uniquely as something that lasts. What can be learned from them? Which of their strategies and secrets can be applied to our lives today and our ambitions for tomorrow? How can such treasures enrich us still?

For the past two years I've been a student of cathedrals. I visited the great cathedral of Milan and studied the history of its construction. Washington National Cathedral in Washington, D.C., opened its doors to me and generously made its staff available for questions. I've spent many days at the Cathedral of St. John the Divine in New York. I've recalled my visits to the Duomo in Florence, and to Chartres and Notre Dame. Each can be counted among the most remarkable man-made structures on the planet.

There is a special feeling that comes with entering any

one of them. It is definite and distinct. It's a feeling inside the chest palpable enough to be physical. First, the sharp intake of breath. The cool, damp scent of ancient marble can be inhaled like a mist. You take a few steps, but only a few, and then you stop. Your eyes adjust to the light. You look up as the cathedral builders meant for you to do. The ribbed vaults and buttresses seem to support the weight of the roof effortlessly. You take a few more steps and stop again. You're not sure how to take in everything before you, not sure what to look at first or how long to study it or see it more clearly: the exquisite carvings of the walnut choir stalls with their seventy-one images of the martyrs, the parapet on the south pulpit recalling the heroic feats of Saul and David, the archbishop's magnificent chair, the brilliant stained-glass windows that tell of everything from the life of Saint Ambrose to the story of Samson and the lion. There is almost a measure of regret that what you behold is too great to truly know in the short time you've allotted. The sense of being overwhelmed is finally tempered by the quiet and stillness.

I've tried to understand this feeling and the ingredients that give it such a unique flavor and texture. It's more than aesthetically pleasing art and craftsmanship. I've tried to understand why the feeling embodies both pleasure and power. I think the feeling is about what went into building the cathedral, what you might know about it, what you can imagine, and what you know you can never know or imagine. Stone is stone and glass is glass, but they are not that anymore, not here. There has been a transformation, and it is the transformation that you feel. It stirs something within, touches a life force. The way the cathedral's stone and glass have come to be fit together suggests something monumental, not about the cathedral as a building, but about the act of building it, about the forces of humanity marshaled on behalf of this creation. How powerful would it be to crack the atom of that transformation? What energy would be released? How would it be measured?

We know that when we eat an apple we get energy from it. That energy is measured in calories. As every high school student knows, one of the iron laws of physics is that energy is never created or destroyed, it is only transferred. So the amount of calories, or energy, we get from an apple is equivalent to the amount of calories, or energy, that contributed to growing that apple. All of nature's varied forces that came together to bring apple and tree into creation are there to be savored in the sweet juices that give us strength.

Think of all that went into building a cathedral: muscle, surely; ingenuity, vision, will. Layer upon layer of knowledge—of design, architecture, physics—accumulated over the years and was passed along through generations, energy of almost unmeasurable proportions. Is there any doubt that blood and tears mixed with the sweat that spilled into ancient soil during its centuries of construction, that the builders devoted their entire lives to it without ever being able to see their work finished, or that entire fortunes were sacrificed on its behalf? The story of any single aspect of it—whether the quarrying and transporting of marble hundreds of miles in ox carts and on the

backs of men, or the painstaking chiseling of the master
sculptors and their apprentices—would read like an epic
saga. And so it surrounds us like an enormous gift that we
can never repay, a gift not of architecture but of humanity.
This is what we're feeling, what catches our breath. We
become custodians of a bond between ourselves and the
people who shared and sacrificed for our pleasure and
benefit. That is what touches and transforms us, what
quickens the beat of our own hearts.

This is a book about searching for the spirit of the cathedral builders and using that spirit to make our lives and our
country better. It is about capturing the spirit of the cathedral builders not through the experience of walking into a
glorious cathedral, but through the experience of living,
giving, and serving in a way that builds a cathedral within.
It is about the extraordinary people in America who are
doing this today. Following the basic principles that guided
cathedral builders and committing their life's work to
something larger than themselves, to something so large it
may be unfinishable, they've come to know the unique fulfillment of building a cathedral within. Most important,
they are providing the leadership, lacking until now, to
make a lasting difference in the lives of our children.

Throughout this book you will see numerous examples
of the fundamental principles responsible for the success of
the cathedral builders. These principles are for you if you've
ever wanted to create meaningful change in your community, or if you've ever been on the staff, board, or volunteer
committee of a local nonprofit organization. They are for

you if you've ever had an interest in mentoring, literacy, hunger, poverty, domestic violence, housing, AIDS, education, the environment, health care, or any other social issue. They are for you if you are starting or finishing college, business school, or law school and don't want to choose between creating wealth and serving the public interest, but would rather embrace the challenge of creating community wealth to serve the public interest. They are for you if what you want to do next is "something that counts."

I tend to think of the sections of the book that follows as individual bricks or stained-glass windows, the raw material of cathedrals. Some are there to illuminate and shed light on a person or idea you might want to examine more closely. Others can be picked up like building blocks, fit together, and fashioned to suit your purpose as you build something of your own. I have not sought the journalist's distance or detachment from the people you'll meet in the pages that follow. In fact, I've done just the opposite. Some are colleagues whose work I've long admired, sought to understand better, and thought important to share.

Of the many lessons to be learned from the cathedral builders, there are at least five fundamental overarching principles that can give meaning and purpose to our lives, help our work endure, and make our communities stronger:

1. Devoting your life to a cause you will never see completed need not diminish your craftsmanship and dedication. Cathedral builders worked backward from a grand

vision and a detailed blueprint that, if followed, would produce the desired outcome.

2. Cathedral building requires the sharing of strength, the contribution of not just the artisans and experts, but of everyone in the community. Ambitious civic projects can't be achieved by government, business, or religious institutions alone. They require all of civic society.

3. The great cathedrals are built, literally, upon the foundations of earlier efforts. The effort to incorporate the work that came before is conscious and deliberate, and the cathedrals are stronger, more solid, and better built for it.

4. Cathedrals were sustained and maintained because they actually generated their own wealth and support. The main source of funding for their building or renovation was income from accumulated land and property. In this way, cathedrals did not just rely on donations, handouts, or redistributed wealth, but instead created new community wealth.

5. Cathedrals, through their stained-glass panels, statues, and paintings, were intentionally designed to convey stories and values to people who were otherwise illiterate. In this way, they taught important history, passed along best practices, and perpetuated a philosophy and culture that reflected their values.

The aspiration to be part of something bigger and more lasting than ourselves is universal in human nature. It is not beyond the reach of either research or instruction. It has applicability in many fields. In the mid-1990s a consistent bestseller, translated into a number of languages, was a business book called *Built to Last*. The authors, Jim Collins and Jerry Porras, studied the great visionary and enduring companies like Hewlett-Packard, Motorola, Disney, and 3M, among others. They found that their leaders were not just good "time tellers" but were "clock builders" who institutionalized greatness. They identified the key lessons and strategies of leaders responsible for companies "built to last." One fundamental distinguishing characteristic of such leaders is that they "preserve a cherished core ideology while simultaneously stimulating progress and change in everything that is not part of their core ideology." There are other ingredients as well, such as setting "Big Hairy Audacious Goals," and careful attention to succession planning.

Many of Porras and Collins's findings appeal beyond the corporate world and have been wisely embraced by visionary and entrepreneurial nonprofit organizations as well. Their utility and applicability in that sector are unquestioned, but fundamentally, they were developed to explain the success of enterprises that create shareholder wealth. As a result, the "built to last" framework, while instructive, is too limited.

When the objective shifts from creating shareholder wealth to creating community wealth, the lessons of

Collins and Porras's clock builders pale in comparison to the lessons of cathedral builders. Indeed, there's probably not a clock anywhere in the world built to last as long as the great Gothic cathedrals that continue to grace the sites on which they were constructed centuries ago. That is why, at this moment in history, our country desperately needs the lessons of the cathedral builders to create a better future for the next generation. Those building the cathedral within will want to apply those lessons too.

III

Once, when I was no more than nine or ten years old, my best friend and I worked in the cool, damp basement of my family's old house in Pittsburgh to build an airplane. Not a model airplane. A real airplane. It was an ambitious undertaking. We devoted our entire summer vacation to the job. We both sunk all of our allowance into it. Then, as now, airplane parts for 737s were quite expensive. So, in addition to the fact that we knew nothing about building airplanes, early on we faced the classic dilemma: We couldn't buy the materials we needed, so instead we bought the materials we could afford. The airplane never flew.

Many of those working for social change in America are unfortunately forced to approach their task in the same counterstrategic way. I know this because I have been part of that effort for the past twenty years, and I know that unless we change, we are destined to suffer the same result. Available funds are so inadequate against the magnitude of problems that all of our well-meaning organizations are forced to focus on whatever short-term strategies we can afford, rather than the long-term strategies that are most needed. In the antihunger field, the result is dollar after dollar spent on larger and more efficient food banks, canned-food drives, soup kitchens, community gardens, and other measures that relieve hunger, but woefully little targeted at preventing hunger or attacking the root cause of hunger, which is poverty. Without substantially more resources devoted to community development, economic opportunity, advocacy, job training and readiness, and education, the effort to end hunger, like the airplane in my basement, simply won't get off the ground.

The most committed and thoughtful social-change activists, those upon whom our society depends to solve social problems, are forced to spend most of their time and energy raising money to support their work, rather than devoting their ingenuity, problem-solving skills, and other talents to devising effective strategies and programs. This is as true for presidents of large universities as it is for founders of neighborhood soup kitchens. Donors have to be solicited over and over again and foundations reapplied to. The debilitating cycle of hand-to-mouth funding interrupts and ruins program execution. Imagine driving a car cross-country but having to stop and get gas only one gallon at a time. The car would surely break down before completing the journey. Yet that's the way we expect non-profit organizations to operate.

For ten years I've enjoyed a privilege and responsibility through Share Our Strength I would never have dreamed possible. I've signed checks totaling more than $60 million for hundreds of organizations across the United States working to feed children, provide health care, end hunger, reverse poverty, and support families in need. Each of those organizations was carefully selected for doing work in its community that is not only caring and compassionate, but efficient and effective. Sixty million dollars can do a lot of good, and it has. I've been to the schools where we started breakfast programs and seen the kids who once started class hungry but are now paying attention and learning to read. I've been to the health clinics we've built and seen children growing who once might have perished. But the satisfaction of raising and distributing such critically needed funds is tempered by disappointment and the realization that our best effort so far is not good enough. There are still too many children we do not reach. Any honest appraisal demands that we change course.

There is more hunger in the United States today than when we began. More children live in poverty and danger. Our funds are building sand castles that can't withstand the rising tide, that are certain to be eroded, if not swept away. Anyone working on issues affecting children, from literacy and education to child abuse and welfare, harbors the same disconcerting emotions. Simply to keep going stubbornly in the same direction would be both naive and wasteful, not just for Share Our Strength, of course, but for the entire national community of nonprofit organizations, many working in tandem with well-intentioned government programs. This doesn't mean we should stop building, only that we need different materials and a new architecture.

Come to think of it, I must not have had much confidence that the airplane I tried to build so many years ago would actually fly. If I had, I would probably have built it outdoors rather than in my basement. Now, at the age of forty-four, I am more committed than ever to finishing what I started when I created Share Our Strength in 1984. But I am also more certain that we simply cannot "get there from here." We need to raise our sights higher and search for new ways to reach our vision.

Cathedral builders were, of course, searchers themselves, and the places they built are the places people come in search of answers. Searchers congregate. There is intimacy there. Searching exposes your needs; nothing could be more personal, or more universal. So the search for the spirit of the cathedral builders is the story of my search, too.

It is a search that has taken me in many directions. It is said that the pharaoh's tombs inside the pyramids at Giza go down as deep as the pyramids are high. I know that in the Washington National Cathedral, the four mammoth piers that soar 98 feet overhead are built from bases so deep within the cathedral that they are actually 324 feet tall. A prerequisite of building out and up is to begin by digging down deep and within.

In eighth grade at the public high school I attended growing up in Pittsburgh, I had an English teacher named Mr. Klieger. He was a large man, tall and broad, with close-cropped hair and glasses that made his sleepy eyes look larger than they were. Against his size, the contrast of his mild manner seemed even more accentuated. He loved literature, and greeted us on the first day of school sitting quietly at his desk with this quote scrawled across the blackboard: "Words signify man's refusal to accept the world as it is." I can't remember who the line is from, but I have thought often about how many times words are used for that reason.

I find myself refusing to accept the world as it is. I'm not just speaking of hunger, poverty, injustice, and the need for social change. What I refuse to accept is the narrow range of choices for thinking about such issues, the traditional either/or's that circumscribe so many of our choices before we've even made them. And so I've been a seeker, not of fortune, glory, or the holy grail, but of new ideas, common grounds, and unexpected intersections of interest. The painter Eugène Delacroix once wrote that what inspires great artists "is not new ideas, but their obsession with the idea that what has already been said is still not enough." Cathedral builders must have believed that what had already been was still not enough.

Twenty years have passed since I first came to Washington seeking a way to leave some mark on the world, to leave it different than I found it. It was late spring of 1977 when I borrowed my mother's Ford Grenada and drove to Washington from Philadelphia the day after my graduation from the University of Pennsylvania. I was determined to intern on Capitol Hill until someone in Congress hired me. Originally, I thought having a hand in drafting the law of the land was the way to make a difference that would last. In a staff position in the U.S. Senate, I set myself to the task at hand with unequaled ardor, learning the parliamentary rules of the Senate, practicing how to count votes, and drafting countless bills and amendments, sometimes two a day, to do everything from establishing tax credits for solar energy adaptations to increasing appropriations for school lunch. Years often went by before a measure became law, if it ever did at all. But even when bills survive the committee process and all of the political machinations they face and are finally enacted, they can be repealed by other laws or rendered moot by events.

Both of the senators for whom I worked ended up running for president—a popular pastime in the U.S. Senate. Neither Gary Hart nor Bob Kerrey ended up getting their party's presidential nomination, but the temptation of presidential politics shifted my focus to the power of leadership embodied in a single voice. Powerful as it can be, though, that chosen voice is sometimes drowned out. First it must be chosen, but even then it sometimes fails. Four presidents have passed through the White House over two decades. More than a hundred men put themselves forward for the job. The words of few are on the lips of schoolchildren today.

I didn't leave government disappointed or a disbeliever. I left with a new awareness of its limitations and a conviction that what I'd learned there would have an impact in the nonprofit sector.

Twenty years is too short a period to bestow wisdom, but too long not to have learned anything at all. One central lesson I've learned is that social science is far too narrow a discipline with which to address social problems, especially problems concerning children. Bart Harvey, president of The Enterprise Foundation, which has worked to help neighborhood-based organizations and local residents revitalize some of the most distressed communities in this country, explains: "We are frequently asked, 'What will it take to change conditions in the inner city?' The answer to that question depends on how we answer another, more deeply rooted, quandary. What are our obligations to each other in this, one of the greatest, democratic, free-enterprise systems the world has ever seen?"

The greatest truths are timeless, as are the spirits of those who teach them. On March 3, 1968, about a month before he died, the Reverend Martin Luther King, Jr., delivered a sermon at Ebenezer Baptist Church in Atlanta. For three generations, his family's history had been entwined with this redbrick church. He joined when he was five, and was ordained there at nineteen. Both his father and grandfather had been pastors. The sermon he delivered that morning, at the same podium from which he'd delivered his first sermon and would deliver his last, was about King David's ambition to build a great temple, one of the most significant challenges facing the Hebrew people.

Dr. King read what he described as "not one of the most familiar passages" from the Old Testament. The "overlooked" passage from the eighth chapter of First Kings reads: "And it was in the heart of David my father to build an house of the name of the Lord God of Israel. And the Lord said unto David my father, 'Whereas it was in thine heart to build an house unto my name, thou didst well that it was within thine heart.' "

King asked the congregation to contemplate the phrase "Thou didst well that it was within thine heart." This was what he really wanted to talk about that morning. His interpretation of the phrase was that God had spoken "as if to say, 'David, you will not be able to finish the temple. You will not be able to build it. But I just want to bless you, because it was within thine heart.' "

King went on to catalog leaders from Gandhi to Woodrow Wilson to the apostle Paul, all of whom had not lived to see the fulfillment of their dreams. Slowly but powerfully, he built to this conclusion: "So many of us in life start out building temples: temples of character, temples of justice, temples of peace. And so often we don't finish them. Because life is like Schubert's Unfinished Symphony. At so many points we start, we try, we set out to build our various temples. And I guess one of the great agonies of life is that we are constantly trying to finish that which is unfinishable. . . . Well, that is the story of life. And the thing that makes me happy is that I can hear a voice crying through the vista of time saying, 'It may not come today or it may not come tomorrow, but it is well that it is within thine heart. It's well that you are trying. You may not see it. The dream may not be fulfilled, but it's just good that you have a desire to bring it into reality. It's well that it's in thine heart.' "

King's temple "in thine heart" was really just another way of describing "the cathedral within." It was a frequent theme of his sermons. It must have been what he meant when, on another occasion, he said, "Everyone can be great because everyone can serve. All it takes is a heart full of grace, and a soul that generates love." The pages that follow are dedicated to those with hearts full of grace.

CHAPTER TWO

Starting Points

Our overriding goal ought to be to save the children. Other goals—reducing the cost of welfare, discouraging illegitimacy, and preventing long-term welfare dependency—are all worthy. But they should be secondary to the goal of improving the life prospects of the next generation.

—William Julius Wilson, social scientist

I

On September 30, 1998, my son, Zach, became a teenager, a status he has long coveted.

Thirteen probably sounds young to you—not many years, a baker's dozen, still a mere child. Zach, however, has taken a more entrepreneurial approach to childhood. His preteen career has been marked by innovation and experimentation. What you might measure in years, some of us have had to cope with one day at a time, and there have been 4,745 of those days, each one's safe passage a celebration of sorts. As certainly as they go by quickly, it is a lot of them.

At thirteen, Zach sleeps late. His legs hurt. He invites

girls to movies. He listens to rap and rock. He lights matches. He makes his own sandwiches. He changes faster than a Compaq laptop can document. That's what kids do, of course. They change. Mostly, they change from one stage of childhood to another, but at thirteen, there's another dimension. He is still a boy, but no longer just a boy, no longer all boy. And of course he is not yet a man. He is on the cusp of manhood.

His room is littered with evidence of sweet paradox: part museum to childhood, part laboratory of the future. The radio blasting alternative rock is plugged into the same outlet as his night-light. The hockey trophies on his dresser tower over miniature Playmobil figures that he still arranges and rearranges like a general deploys troops on a battlefield. Next to the shoulder pads of his hockey gear lies a Mickey Mouse T-shirt. The room is a collage of his interests, development, and growth, a time capsule of the last twelve years. Like a crime scene cordoned off and untouched, it is rich with as much telling evidence as any witness's words. Most revealing of all is what it says not just about who this child is, but what he needs.

Like Zach, the room is still a work in progress. Over time, the blue-checked wallpaper has been covered over by posters, sports jerseys, T-shirts, magazine photos, bumper stickers, expired license plates, street signs, and hats.

On the wall across from his bed is the Andy Warhol poster of Superman that I bought at the Museum of Modern Art in 1989, when Zach was four years old. It was the first item put up on the now crowded walls and the

only one put there by me. Superman is descending from
the top lefthand corner, cape aflutter, blowing a huge puff
of white air onto billowing gray clouds of smoke. There are
words coming out of his mouth in a black-bordered bal-
loon. "Let me tell you what he's saying without looking,"
Zach will boast, squeezing his eyes shut. "'Good! A mighty
puff of my super-breath extinguished the forest fire.'" He
gets it verbatim. I can imagine how many nights he fell
asleep staring at it, an entire adventure unfolding in his
mind. I know I got my money's worth from this poster.

Next to Superman is a poster of the entire Super
Bowl XXXI Championship Green Bay Packer football
team. Four hockey jerseys are thumbtacked to the walls,
sleeves spread wide like an old friend's greeting, enough of
them to join Zach in making up a full five-man team. One
shirt has Pittsburgh Penguin great Mario Lemieux's number 66, another says TURCOTTE STICKHANDLING SCHOOL.
There are also mounted action photos of Lemieux and his
teammate Jaromir Jagr, and full-color magazine pictures of
Michael Jordan at the basketball hoop and Pittsburgh Pirate
legend Roberto Clemente with bat ready to explode in a
swing across the plate. The front of a Wheaties box featuring the 1991 NHL Champion Pittsburgh Penguins is
nailed to the adjoining wall. The arms of the players are
raised to hoist the Stanley Cup over their heads as they
skate a victory lap.

If nature has taught us anything universal, it is that kids
tell us, by showing us, what they need. Zach could not be
more explicit if he'd taken out want ads in *The Washington*

Post. Kids need heroes. They need someone to look up to. They need to believe in strength over weakness, in success over failure. They want proof that practice and hard work lead to achievement. They need positive role models to keep their compass needles pointing in the right direction. Zach has all but erected a highway billboard to advertise his pitch.

That's not all this room has to tell. Two battalions of soldiers, not two inches high, face off across from each other on top of the chest of drawers. It is what Zach, since the age of four or five, has called a "setup." A battle is raging, and only Zach knows where and why and how. Every formation comes with a new story.

Zach's night table is crowded with fourteen small hockey trophies stacked under a shelf holding additional trophies for swimming and baseball. They are a measure of success. In the corner of the room, hidden by his open door, more than two dozen broken hockey sticks are propped against the wall, as if to say: Here too lives a hero, albeit a young and aspiring one.

The night table also holds the one lamp used to light the room. It is within arm's reach of his bed, which was my bed as a child growing up in Pittsburgh. The base for the bulb and shade is an admiral, sharply dressed in red, white, and blue, standing at attention on top of what could be a drum with patriotic draping. Shoulders squared, hands tight to the side, his steadfastness is beyond question. The lamp is more than thirty-five years old and has been rewired twice. When I turn it off after tucking him in each night, I'm twisting the same switch that my dad twisted after tucking me in, and leaving the same loyal sentry there on watch.

At times, self-awareness sneaks up on Zach like a cat brushing a leg. One afternoon while kneeling at a table in the family room, he's building a fort out of Legos. The phone rings. It is a girl from school who likes him. If there is a conversation under way, she's carrying it. He is monosyllabic. I feel for her. Afterward, he puts down the phone and smiles. He looks up from his toys, half understanding and half not, and says: "I've got girls calling me, Dad, and I'm still playing with Legos."

Writing about one's own children is fraught with danger for many reasons, not least of which is that what one parent cares about or thinks important, others may not. But writing about children only in the abstract has its dangers, too. Thinking of children in the abstract is part of the problem in the first place. There is nothing on the planet more real to me than Zach and his sister, Mollie.

Of all the times to write about my son, this is the one that feels right, not only because the changes he's going through are so pronounced, but because he is more than halfway to adulthood. I've helped get him there, and like the driver of an eighteen-wheeler hauling a precious load cross-country, I am finally past the midpoint. That's not to say I can take one hand off of the wheel. He hasn't even entered high school yet, so of course there are plenty of

dangerous curves yet to come; some of the darkest high-
ways and steepest hills lie ahead. I can't even pretend to
know what the rest of the journey will be like, but at least
the Continental Divide is in my rearview mirror and I'm
comfortable at the wheel. No coasting allowed. No cruise
control. But if there's a time to pull over at a rest stop,
unfold the map, and retrace the trip thus far, that time is
now.

Zach turned thirteen just in time for his weeklong
eighth-grade field trip to New York. On a cool, wet fall
morning right after his birthday, I woke him at 5:30 A.M.,
an hour earlier than usual. It is hard to get used to the
effort required to wake him. The St. Patrick's Day parade
could march through his room without disturbing him. He
was stretched across a bed that seems to shrink more each
week. I squeezed a bare shoulder, flopped his wrist, and
eventually shook him until he got out of bed and, without
saying a word, walked into the bathroom.

We weren't going to the bus stop, but rather directly to
school to meet the special touring buses for New York. It
seemed awfully far away for him to be on his own, knowing
the kind of mischief he gets into when he's just in the next
aisle at the grocery store. Of course, there were teachers as
chaperons, but there were only six or eight of them, and
that may not have been a fair match.

Zach was too tired to shower and not hungry enough to
eat, so we jumped into the Jeep, where he immediately
turned on the radio, almost in synchronization with my
turning the ignition. I was grateful for this indication that

he was breathing and conscious. He was quiet until we got to school. Shouting over the radio, I told him about his grandfather's 1911 arrival at Ellis Island, since that's where the school trip would begin. Then there would be a tour of the Lower East Side, the New York Stock Exchange, Central Park, Broadway, and more.

We got to the school's parking lot by 6:00 A.M. Two large touring buses were loading. Zach opened the back door of the Jeep and grabbed the backpack that had been stuffed with clothes, a disposable camera, and Snickers bars. He started to run off, but I yelled, "Hey!" He turned back and we touched fists, the bottom of his to the top of mine, like a basketball player coming off the court with his replacement coming off the bench. It's one of our few permissible public displays of affection.

He ran off to join his friends while I stood around with the other parents for about a half hour waiting for the buses to depart. Zach never looked back or over again. He was either unaware of my presence or oblivious to it. Maybe he had just grown familiar and comfortable with always being watched, the way a president or celebrity learns to ignore the press and paparazzi.

Through the large windows of the touring bus, I saw him find a seat at the back. He pointed to something that made his buddies laugh. He seemed relaxed but acutely aware of the reactions of his peers. He pulled his baseball cap down tighter on his head. He teased a girl with a blond ponytail in the seat ahead of him so that she grabbed his hand and then he her wrist. The teasing stopped and the conversation shifted. Both held on a few seconds longer than necessary.

Outside, a few of the kids who arrived late checked in and then ran over to give their parents a farewell hug. There was no kissing, or even eye contact. The drizzle got a bit stronger, and a deep chill seeped in for those of us who had been standing around for more than thirty minutes. We shifted our feet and plunged hands deeper into pockets. Having waited so long, no one wanted to leave before the buses did, but there were other kids to drive to school, jobs to get to, and traffic to avoid. Eighth graders don't sit still long. If you take your eye off of any one, you need to work a moment to relocate them, sometimes finding their friends first, like locating a special star by recognizing the constellation it helps comprise. I tried to keep my eye on Zach.

The night before, I had sat on the edge of his bed and talked to Zach about New York's dangers and the necessary precautions. I said nothing of my own eighth-grade class trip to New York. After all, that was back in 1969. What did he need to know of my losing forty dollars to a ticket scalper, of Kathleen Shinhoffen knocking on the door of my hotel room after midnight? I spoke instead of strangers and crowds, of pickpockets and con men, of drugs and alcohol, even of sex and condoms. It wasn't quite fire and brimstone, but it was close.

He was no more overtly attentive than usual. Eyes glued to the TV, he worked the remote with one hand and stuffed a sandwich into his mouth with the other. Only one of the topics I raised was even remotely interesting to him. I'd known it would be and had intentionally thrown it in like bait to hook him: pickpockets. "Here's how they work, Dad. In teams. One of them creates a distraction . . ." He held forth at great length on the nuances involved. Somewhat alarmingly, his knowledge seemed to be state-of-the-art. I hope he understands condoms as well when he needs to.

Out in the parking lot that next morning, in the misty twilight before dawn, the teachers were not easy to distinguish from the students. At six-foot-one, Zach's well-dressed friend Joey looked older than his five-foot-three media teacher, Ms. Lee, clad in tennis shorts and T-shirt. I recognized her and world studies teacher Mr. Goldberg. Zach had not had an easy year with them. Their names were familiar and inextricably linked to the large, seven-dollar bucket of golf balls Zach and I split at the driving range just the previous weekend. Zach would carefully reach down to balance a ball on the tee, step back and raise the iron club high over his left shoulder, stop, flash a Jack Nicholson grin, and say, "Hello there, Mr. Goldberg's little head." Then he'd whack the hell out of that ball.

Finally, the buses were fully loaded and the luggage stowed. The kids were counted one last time. The bus drivers could be seen fastening their own seat belts. Parents sought out their children one last time for that all-important send-off wave and the attempted look in the eye that repeated in silent but unmistakable code whatever their most fervent warning had been.

As the engines turned over and the wheels began to roll, every parent's arm waved in a great arc. I can report with certainty that not a single student waved back or interrupted their conversation to look up or out the window.

A collective sigh went up from the parents as they looked at each other and shrugged in chagrin. We'd been found out. Our covers were blown. We had not been standing there that whole time for the children after all, but rather for ourselves. They were fine. They were oblivious. If not for the fact that they were our flesh and blood, we might as well have been standing on another planet. We headed back to our cars.

It has been said that at precisely this point in their development, when our children seem to need us the least, they actually need us the most. This is either one of the last of the great delusions that parents feel bound to defend, or a profound truth that, like all profound truths, must be accepted on faith. Either way, the work remains unfinished. Thirteen years—4,745 days—are just a few truckloads of bricks, enough to start a cathedral, perhaps, but not to finish one.

The day that began in one parking lot with Zach at 6:00 A.M. ended eighteen hours later with a reminder of him, in another, more unusual parking lot. I was supposed to fly to Dallas for an annual Share Our Strength fundraising dinner at Star Canyon, one of the best restaurants in the country. But our plane ran into thunderstorms and high winds. Air traffic control put us into a holding pattern for so long that we ran out of fuel. We diverted to Austin, where there was not a single spare gate at the terminal. Instead, we parked about a mile away, where we sat for five hours in 87-degree heat with other parked planes on the tarmac.

Every seat was filled, and I was in 9B, a middle seat! A marine sat to my right, and on my left was an elderly woman who asked more questions than Zach and Mollie. The passengers were restless, particularly so because of those others that could be seen being off-loaded by ambulance from the plane parked next to ours. Heat stroke, we guessed. Maybe claustrophobia.

By 7:00 P.M., the sun was setting. We were still stranded away from the terminal building, which in the shimmering heat beckoned like Oz. It was clear I would miss the dinner at Star Canyon. Other passengers were missing their meetings too, and worse, their connections to other destinations. Complimentary wine was being poured in every row, and those minibottles of scotch and vodka were quickly consumed. The plane looked trashed, newspapers and garbage up and down the center aisle. The passengers who had drunk too much were spilling what was left of their drinks on other passengers. Misery and free booze make for a dangerous combination on a packed plane.

When the side door of the plane was opened to let in some air, a few of us stood carefully at the threshold, looking across to the other planes that had parked nearby. The passengers across the way looked just as tired and hungry. For the second time that day, I was in a group that was waving to people who did not wave back.

This one storm in Texas wreaked havoc on the entire air traffic control system. Connecting flights to the West Coast were being missed and eventually canceled. Passengers at the other end waiting for those flights were as out of luck as if they were in the eye of the storm. Airline crews were not able to get to the airports at which they were based. Though the weather could have cleared, we were warned that our pilots were about to reach the FAA's limit on hours worked in a single day. They would soon "go illegal," and planes would have to wait for replacement crews to be flown in.

The complete unraveling we experienced is what scientists specializing in chaos theory call "Sensitive Dependence on Initial Conditions" (SDIC). It's the snowball that triggers the avalanche. The same principle explains why leaving for work ten minutes later than usual doesn't mean getting there ten minutes late, but possibly falling an entire hour behind if the ten-minute delay plunges you into rush-hour traffic, complete with accidents and detours.

As science writer James Gleick describes in his bestseller *Chaos: Making a New Science*, "Traditionally, when physicists saw complex results, they looked for complex causes. The modern study of chaos began with the creeping realization in the 1960s that quite simple mathematical equations could model systems every bit as violent as a waterfall. Tiny differences in input could quickly become overwhelming differences in output. . . . Errors and uncertainties multiply, cascading upward through a chain of turbulent features. . . . In science as in life, a chain of events can have a point of crisis that could magnify small changes."

Sensitive Dependence on Initial Conditions. Airplanes are vulnerable to it. Children are too. For example, scientists now have a new understanding of the critical role that sufficient nutrition plays in guaranteeing normal development of the fetus, ensuring that infants get the nutrients they need to develop their brains and neurological systems and to avoid low birth weight.

The body's organs don't all grow at the same time. Each organ undergoes its own specific growth period. If a nutrition deficiency, or what doctors call a "nutritional insult," occurs during a time when a certain organ needs to be growing, the damage can be incalculable and irreversible. This is because an organ grows in two ways: when its cells divide, and when its cells increase in size.

Some organs—the kidneys and liver, for instance—are classified as "renewing" or "expanding," which means they can make up growth at a later stage. Others, like the brain or nervous system, are static, which means that at some point, sometimes at a very early stage, their cells permanently lose the capacity to divide. At birth, the brain is approximately 60 percent developed. At six months, it has grown to 90 percent of its full size. The remaining growth takes place between six and eighteen months. At that point, the brain is fully grown. If it isn't, there is unfortunately nothing that can be done to cause brain tissue cells to further divide to make up for lost brain growth. The cells that are already there will expand and grow, but there will never be more of them, never as many as in the brain of a child whose minimal nutritional requirements were satisfied.

Sensitive Dependence on Initial Conditions. The most common nutritional problem in the United States today is anemia due to iron depletion. This is particularly common in late infancy and early childhood. Iron sits at the center of a red blood cell and is what the oxygen taken in through the lungs attaches itself to. Less iron means less oxygen circulating to the body's organs. I've never thought of hunger as suffocation, but in this way, it is. Anemic children weigh less and are shorter, as you might expect. They also have shorter attention spans, less ability to concentrate, and less curiosity. There are communities within urban areas of the United States where 100 percent of the population is anemic by medical standards. Inadequate nutrition in the formative early years between birth and age three can irrevocably affect brain growth, learning potential, long-term health, academic performance, and employment potential.

Sensitive Dependence on Initial Conditions. Neurobiological events and conditions from the very first moments of life have a profound impact on learning abilities forever after. Nutrition, nurturing, and an enriched and stimulating environment actually affect and alter the physical structure, nerve cells, synapses, and blood vessels of the brain itself. For example, at a conference of neuroscientists outside of Baltimore in 1990, Dr. Michael Leon, a professor of psychobiology at the University of California, told a small group of us that one thing every infant learns in its very first days out of the womb is how to find its mother's breast. It is olfactory learning based on maternal odor. The region of the brain that processes olfactory learning experiences an increase in the number of cells surrounding it. This may be due to increased cell division or to an increased number of neurons. Either way, there is no question that such learning alters the structure of the brain.

Sensitive Dependence on Initial Conditions. The vast bulk of public and private resources is invested today at the wrong end of the life cycle. Nothing is more cost effective than early intervention. As a society, we spend decades paying for programs designed to compensate for a few months of neglect. A short period of time at the very beginning of a child's life represents a large opportunity to provide the nurturing, health care, environment, and nutrition that make a permanent difference. It is almost as if nature were saying, "Pay attention to this very critical development stage. Put the necessary resources into the right time and place at the very start, and the healthy bodies and minds that result will pay dividends for a lifetime." It's hard to imagine a better deal.

The chaos that results from air traffic delays pales in comparison to that caused by developmental delays in children. It just takes longer to see. Sensitive Dependence on Initial Conditions is at the heart of both. As both chaos expert James Gleick and child development experts document, "Errors and uncertainties multiply, cascading upward through a chain of turbulent features."

Whether teenagers on a bus to New York or at-risk kids in Baltimore or Harlem, children remain children until they are adults.

For Zach, that leaves 2,920 days to go.

II

Earlier this year, while sitting with my laptop computer at a table in the café car of an Amtrak train from Washington, D.C., to New York, I started to reread a report published by the Carnegie Corporation of New York called "Starting Points: Meeting the Needs of Our Youngest Children." The goal of the report was to use scientific evidence to enhance the credibility of an agenda for the healthy development of children from birth through age three. I had only a few hours to digest it and write a memo for the Share Our Strength staff.

I was at work for all of about seven seconds when a young boy sat down across from me with his backpack and the cardboard tray of food he had just purchased. He was black, and looked sad and lonely. The conductor, who had walked the boy to this seat because he was traveling alone, asked him to wait right there at the end of the trip, until someone brought his uncle to him. "Do not leave the train on your own. You'll never find your uncle at Penn Station in New York. It's too crowded." The boy just nodded. He stared out the large picture window and tried hard not to look interested in the passing scenery.

I smiled at the boy but started typing again as fast as I could. He pulled a fresh deck of cards from the cardboard tray, tore off the cellophane wrapping, and stretched his neck to peer over the top of my computer screen. "You know how to play cards?" he asked. It didn't matter to him whether I was fourteen or forty. Boys his age—I was guessing twelve—view most everyone they meet as potential playmates. They are the human equivalent of puppies.

Since I travel so much, I usually try to resist the notion that I have an obligation to be companionable to whomever fate puts in the seat near mine. How would I ever get any work done? "Yeah, I know how to play, but I've got lots of homework here." I was trying to put it in terms he'd understand. I smiled to take away the edge.

Then we were both silent. He was hopeful, but I needed the time to work. I'd been counting on it. Every hour I carve out for writing gets taken away for one good reason or another, but a train ride should be inviolate.

I kept typing, but then looked over at him. He looked back at me as if he'd never expected much in the first place. He was wearing a long orange T-shirt with the sleeves cut off and a YOUTH BASKETBALL logo on it. His arms and legs were long, their muscles just developing. His Adidas were untied, just like Zach's always were. Something made me certain he was exactly Zach's age.

I went back to reading the Carnegie report about how adults must give more of themselves to kids, about the patience and persistence they require, and about how we need to take responsibility for all children, not just our own. Of course, it was impossible not to recognize how the report's topic paralleled the predicament that had developed between me and my card-playing friend.

"Okay, just a couple of hands," I said, and reached over for the deck. "What's your name, anyhow?"

"Ernest," he answered, keeping his grip on the cards. Then he split the deck and shuffled it as if he'd been dealing in Las Vegas since he was three. He'd finished school for the year, he told me, and was on his way to spend the week with his uncle in New Jersey.

"Do you want to play war or something?" I asked, underestimating him.

"I was thinking blackjack," he said.

We played a few hands and then switched to poker, first five-card and then seven. He won all but one hand.

"How old are you, Ernest?"

"Twelve," he told me. And I knew that he was.

The blue and green borders on the Carnegie report's cover are appealing to the eye, and they frame a photo of a young girl who is maybe two years old. She has a thick head of curly hair—ringlets coiled both tight and loose—and eyes as large as ripe black plums. There's a bright white spot near the center of each pupil that must be the reflection of the photographer's flash. If the photo were enhanced, the photographer himself and the rest of the room would likely be visible in those dark pupils. It suggests how much more we'd be able to see if we looked at the world through her eyes. Her arm is gripping a small white box that could include anything from crayons to lunch. She looks neither hungry nor sick, but the expression on her face says that she needs us anyway, underscoring the essential point of the document. She is adorable, and her anxious but hopeful face makes it all but impossible to set the report aside.

The first chapter is called "The Quiet Crisis." Its premise is that, in the midst of unprecedented affluence in the United States today, the crucially formative years of early childhood are a time of great risk and loss for millions of children. The period from prenatal to age three is demonstrably the most formative. Ironically, it is also the most neglected. This is because there are no clearly defined institutions, such as preschools, to serve it.

The basic statistics are familiar. There are twelve million children under the age of three in the United States today. One in four lives in poverty. One in four lives in a single-parent family. Nearly a quarter of all pregnant women in America, many of whom are adolescents, receive little or no prenatal care.

Our society acknowledges these facts but not their consequences. The consequences are that poor children are more likely to have poor health, die during childhood, score lower on standardized tests, have out-of-wedlock births, and experience violent crime.

The paradox of our time is that while wealth is being created at unprecedented levels, it is not reaching those in greatest need. If anything, it has created a complacency, a comfort with the status quo, an assumption that a rising tide will lift all boats. The tragedy is not just that the new wealth does not reach all of the intractable pockets of poverty. The tragedy is that prosperity also hides poverty. Just as it may ameliorate it, so can it mask it. It can disguise the deficits children encounter when their most basic needs go unmet. It can blind those who are in a position to offer help to those who need them the most.

The report calls this a "quiet crisis" and explains, "Babies seldom make the news: They do not commit crimes, do drugs, or drop out of school." Low-income parents have little economic clout. Children's early experience is in the home—a realm considered private by policymakers and in which they are reluctant to intrude. What the report tries to emphasize is that "researchers have thoroughly documented the importance of the pre- and postnatal months and the first three years, but a wide gap remains between scientific knowledge and social policy."

Our policies lag behind our knowledge. They do not reflect what scientists have learned about early brain development or the factors that protect young children from risk. Brain development before age one is even more rapid and extensive than previously realized. Although brain cell formation is virtually complete before birth, brain maturation is far from over. The formation of connections among these cells, known as synapses, is the next challenge. Up to fifteen thousand synapses per neuron must be formed to allow learning to take place. In the months after birth, the number of synapses increases from 50 trillion to 1,000 trillion—twentyfold!

Our newest and most important knowledge is that factors other than genetic programming affect the brain. Nutrition is one obvious one. Another, less obvious, is experience. Exposure from early infancy to toys, stimulation, and nurturing shows a measurable impact on brain function at ages twelve and fifteen. Knowing this dictates that we nurture children in very different ways than we have before, but we are not yet doing so.

The report makes two other major points that would not be unfamiliar to cathedral builders, whose success in transforming grand visions into lasting reality depended upon a holistic approach:

– "The pivotal institutions are the family, the health care system, the emerging child care system, religious institutions, community organizations, and the media." It's fascinating that a task force of such traditional liberals as constituted this Carnegie Corporation study does not even mention government in this sentence. Instead, the "pivotal institutions" are community-based organizations like Washington, D.C.'s, premier maternal and child health clinic, Mary's Center, Share Our Strength, Boston City Hospital, and other organizations we know. "Because the family is the main provider of the environment of the infant and toddler, it is clear that the family's care of the young child largely determines the child's early progress. *Our attention to supporting the development of the child, therefore, must focus on family members, on their commitment to the child, their availability, and their resources.*" (Italics mine.)

— In families under stress, problems do not come singularly, and they are linked in complex ways. Neither the problems facing families, nor the solutions to those problems, can be neatly compartmentalized. Any proposed solutions must rest on comprehensive approaches. No single service system can deal with the multiple problems families face. There cannot be a single federal, state, local, or private-sector solution. Rather, resources and commitments from all of these levels and sectors will be necessary.

The report concludes that there is not one magic answer, no silver bullet, that "the problems we describe are many, and they are massive; not one lends itself to a simple solution." So it selects four starting points that would move the country in the direction of giving all children what they need to reach their full potentials. Those starting points are:

- promoting responsible parenthood
- guaranteeing quality child-care choices
- ensuring good health
- mobilizing communities to support young children and their families

In this way, the report is careful not to set unrealistic expectations. Its recommendations are no more than starting points. There are still a lot of other steps to be prescribed, let alone accomplished.

I wanted to know what impact this report had, and so asked the report's authors about steps taken in response to the report's publication. They pointed mostly to Rob Reiner's well-publicized "I Am Your Child" campaign to increase awareness of this early childhood period. They sounded somewhat embarrassed by the fact that Reiner distorted some of their findings in an effort to simplify them for sound-bite consumption, but grateful nevertheless to have the attention that Reiner's friends, like Robin Williams and Billy Crystal, can produce. There's an impressive list of television specials, public service announcements, and other vehicles of awareness that are a consequence of the report. The response in the policy arena is more vague: "stimulating a dialogue," "designing a national conference," and other steps that sound more like wishful thinking than concrete action.

As much as I admire the Carnegie report, it repeats a mistake common to many such publications. It not only suggests but devotes considerable energy to arguing that there is one specific, definable period—in this case, from birth to the age of three—when a child's needs are more urgent than others. This is not true. The needs of this period are distinct. They are different, but they cannot be set against a child's needs at later periods of life.

I'm sympathetic to what the report's authors are trying to achieve: a set of recommendations that can be implemented and will have the support to be implemented because they help readers and policymakers prioritize and know where to begin. If I had to pick just one period of a child's life in which to intervene intensively, then I'd probably agree that the period of birth through age three is the one, but the philosophy of having to pick just one, seductive as it may be, is ultimately counterproductive and dangerously defeating. Albert Einstein once said, "Everything in life should be made as simple as possible, but not simpler." This is too simple.

Though they are some years apart, it's hard not to hear the two-year-old girl in the Carnegie report's cover photo and my twelve-year-old traveling companion Ernest telling us the same thing. They are not finished. Nor are we. They cannot survive on their own. They need us whether they look like it or not, and that need persists through every stage of the journey—not just at the major crossroads, but for the whole ride.

III

I have a picture, balanced near the corner of the rolltop desk in my study, of Mollie when she was very young, being held by my wife, Bonnie, in front of our house. They are on their way to the swimming pool across the street. Mollie is perched in the crook of Bonnie's arm. She's in her bathing suit, and the wisp of a bright pink bow that can be seen in the back of her hair matches the pink in her cheeks. Her hands meet across the top of Bonnie's left shoulder, fingers curled over the embroidery of Bonnie's blouse in a grip guaranteed to hold her in place. At the time, she was five years old. Today she is nine, but she hasn't let go yet.

In the picture, Mollie's chin is tucked below Bonnie's shoulder, and her big, brown eyes are slanting to the left with a mix of skepticism and caution, the way Humphrey Bogart might look at the Germans from the steps of Rick's Café in *Casablanca*. With one exception, Mollie views everything in the world with a mix of skepticism and caution. The exception is her mother. This instinct regarding her mother is as finely honed as if she were a bear cub, gosling, or kitten. But there is also a mischievousness, born of self-awareness, in Mollie's eyes. If life were a game of tag, Bonnie would be base. Snuggled against her mother's warmth, the look on Mollie's face warns the rest of the world: "You can't get me now."

Mollie's trust is warranted. Bonnie understands her completely, and in ways I can try to imitate but never fully achieve. Watching Bonnie with Mollie is like watching a

sleight-of-hand magician up close. I'd swear I saw everything there was to see, but I still don't understand the
trick. Like the time Bonnie wouldn't back off of fining
Mollie a dollar for burping at the breakfast table despite
Mollie's protestations that she forgot, and her seemingly
heartbroken tears.

"Don't you think you were being a little harsh?" I asked
later that day.

"Not really. Did you see how quickly she ran to her
room to get the dollar? She's seen her brother Zach get
fined for that, and it was very important for her to know
that we love her and care for her enough to punish her the
same way."

She was exactly right, but how did she know?

Mollie puts so much faith in her mom that whatever surplus exists is measured and parceled out frugally, and only
when earned. She made me work hard for my share, and
with reason. In March 1992, shortly before her third
birthday, I had just returned from a series of long trips with
Senator Bob Kerrey's unsuccessful presidential primary
campaign. I had met him nearly ten years before, joined his
Senate staff when he was elected in 1992, and agreed to
help in his travels. Some of the trips lasted six or seven
days, with only a quick stop home to change laundry.
Mollie and I were driving through our Silver Spring neighborhood on the way back from the grocery store one day
after the campaign when, from her car seat in the back, she
said, "Dad, can I ask you a question?"

And then, after a pause, "What street is your house on?"

"What?" I asked, thinking I hadn't heard correctly.

"What street is your house on?"

It was a telltale moment. Although she knew I was her dad, and she knew Bonnie and I were married, she did not know I lived in the same house that she did.

Though I was able to convince her that we resided at the same address, her uncertainty about my place in her life continued and manifested itself in many ways. A skinned knee sent her toppling toward Mom, not me. A question raised by something overheard at school could be saved for hours if necessary, until Mom was around to ask. Her most frequent question became "Where's Mom?"

"What do you need Mom for?"

"I just need her. Where is she?"

"Sweetie, you can tell me what you want."

"Okay, I want Mom."

"I mean, if you'll tell me what you want Mom for, maybe I can get it for you."

"I just want to know where she is."

"I don't know."

"Well, how are you going to be able to get me what I want if you don't even know where my mom is?"

On a similar occasion, Mollie appeared on the steps down from her bedroom during a night that her girlfriend Laura was sleeping over.

"I need Mommy," she scowled.

"Oh no, Molls. Mom is exhausted. We definitely don't want to wake her."

"I need Mommy."

"What do you need her for?"

"Mommy's the only one who knows what to do about it."

"About what?"

"Only Mommy!"

"Mollie, tell me."

"My growing pains," she explained, lifting her brother's old hockey jersey that she sleeps in and pointing to a spot on her shin. "Mommy knows how to make them go away," she insisted, heading for the bedroom where Bonnie was asleep.

Situations like this require quick thinking and a liberal dose of what Bonnie and I call distraction theory.

"Molls, Mom only knows the old way to get rid of growing pains. But there's a new way that even Mom doesn't know about yet."

"There is?"

"Yep, you get back in bed, and I'll be right up." I dashed to the kitchen, and when I got back to her room I was holding a large squirt bottle of Nestlé's chocolate syrup.

"Dad! *What are you doing?*" she asked, wide-eyed.

"Let me see that leg."

"Dad!" She and Laura glanced at each other, unsure whether to be shocked or delighted.

"Trust me, Molls. A little bit of this rubbed into your leg and it will feel better in no time."

"Uh, that's okay, Dad. I think it's better already."

"You sure?"

"Yeah, Dad, I'm sure."

"Okay. Good night."

I turned out the light and closed the door.

"Boy, is your dad crazy," Laura whispered.

I heard them whispering and giggling until they fell asleep.

The most important thing I had to learn about being a dad to Mollie was how to be with her. Children have litmus tests, and they don't always extend you the courtesy of letting you know what they are. Mollie's need was subtle but should have been obvious, given its universality. It was a need for me to be willing to be with her, to be fully present, even in the absence of a specific reason, like an organized activity or play. Especially in the absence of a specific reason, Molly required that I be with her on her terms, even though she couldn't express what those terms were. This, more than anything else, may be what builds trust and self-esteem in a child, and the irony is, it is so easy to do.

Most of my time with Mollie had been organized around doing things: going swimming or to a movie, or taking the dogs for a walk. The more I sensed her distance from me, the more things I tried to do. I was not only trying too hard, I was trying the wrong thing. Psychologists have long understood that this is the way men approach all relationships, not just those with their children. Men organize their relationships around activities from the time they are little boys. They play games together or band together to watch other men play sports. Women, however, seek simply being together, from the time they are little girls. If Mollie and I didn't have some specifically scheduled activity, I would typically work on other chores, read in my study, and make phone calls. From the point of view of maximizing time and being productive, it made perfect sense. When it was time to read her a bedtime story, Bonnie would call me after the rest of the bedtime routine had been completed, and I would walk into her room like a dentist who waited until the patient was cleaned and prepped so he wouldn't have to waste a minute's more time than necessary. It was the way I felt, and I'm sure now it was the way it made her feel too.

And so I had to learn what her mother already knew: how to watch a TV show with Mollie even if it wasn't a show I wanted to watch, how to sit there and watch it without also reading a newspaper or magazine, to be fully present. Mollie didn't want me for what I could give her, for where I could take her, or even for what we could do together. She wanted me for me.

A turning point came one summer evening as she grew increasingly frustrated trying to build a "secret hideout" in the backyard. Our lawn slopes steeply to the fence that keeps our dogs in and the neighbors' dog out. The sun was setting, and she should have been winding down before bed, except the thin slate tiles she tried to prop against each other in a corner of the yard kept falling over. She'd been at it for days and days, sometimes with a neighboring girlfriend, sometimes on her own. Now there would be no secret hideout. When the walls fell over for the last time, cracking as they fell, she burst into tears, and her face contorted to a degree I couldn't ignore.

"You know what you need to make this work, Molls?"

"What?"

"You need about sixty bricks."

"Great, but we don't have sixty bricks."

"But we could get them."

"Where?"

"Home Depot. Get your shoes on and hop in the car. Real quick."

I could tell from how quickly she tied her shoes that this was my shot at winning her over. The Home Depot store about three or four miles from our house offered a greater choice in bricks than could possibly be imagined. Either the company has great customer service or the puzzled look on my face engendered genuine pity, because several employees rushed over to ask if I needed some help. We finally settled on the twenty-three-cents-a-brick variety and got our big, flat, wheeled cart, and then I started to load them, two to four at a time. They were rough and heavy, and I wished I'd brought gloves. After being loaded onto the cart, they would need to be unloaded into the Jeep, and then unloaded yet again at the house. I had my work cut out for me.

"Oh please, let me do that, Dad, please!" Mollie begged.

I couldn't possibly imagine anything more unrealistic. The bricks were heavy, and she would have to use two hands just to pick up one of them. If Mollie did it we would be there forever. I glanced at my watch and tried to keep my resistance in check.

"But, sweetie, they're very heavy."

"Please, Dad, I really want to," she begged again, moving quickly to the pile of bricks and hoisting one with both hands. She lugged it over to the cart and laid it next to the handful I'd placed there.

This was going to take all night.

Mollie walked back to the brick pile and carefully selected another one. She took her time making her choice.

Then I realized she wanted it to take all night.

It was rare for the two of us to have time like this alone together. This was the kind of thing her older brother would usually get to do: impulsive, past bedtime, just the two of us together. Mollie wanted it to last.

I leaned back against one of the wood pallets in the store and took a deep breath. Mollie, working steadily at the bricks, relaxed and became chatty, talking to me about what she'd build, and about school and her girlfriends and her upcoming horseback riding lesson. More than one set of walls came down that evening. What I had seen as a task to finish quickly, so that we could go play with bricks the way I think of as play, she saw as play itself. Twenty-three cents a brick is not a bad price to pay to make your daughter happy. Mollie showed me how it could be done for a lot less than that.

I've always tried to spend time in Mollie's school. Her first elementary school, New Hampshire Estates, went from kindergarten through second grade. Like most public schools, it faced the challenge of educating a diverse group of students, whose foundations in the fundamentals were uneven, in classes that were too large. A committed principal created one excuse after another to bring parents into the school buildings: winter concerts, read-a-book week, young authors conferences, spring concerts, silent auction day, career day. Parental participation correlates to early academic achievement.

There are many reasons I like being in my daughter's school. One is that I like to compare and contrast it with other schools to which my work takes me. One week, shortly after spending a morning in Mollie's school, I went to visit an after-school program in Baltimore called The Door. Share Our Strength sponsored a nutrition education program there, and to help us promote it, the vice president's wife, Tipper Gore, was coming to read a book to the kids. The classroom was just like my daughter's classroom in almost every way, except for one glaring difference. As in Mollie's school, there were aspirational posters on the wall declaring I CAN BE WHATEVER I DREAM I CAN BE, NEVER SETTLE FOR LESS THAN YOUR BEST, and TO ACHIEVE YOUR DREAMS, LEARN YOUR ABCS. There were maps and globes and other colorful learning tools. There were computers. But the one, inescapable contrast was a large stenciled sign on the front door of the classroom:

IF I SEE A GUN, OR ANYTHING THAT LOOKS LIKE A GUN, I WILL NOT PICK IT UP. I WILL GO AND GET AN ADULT. BECAUSE GUNS CAN HURT ME. AND I WANT TO BE SAFE.

I try to imagine what it must feel like as a parent to drop off a child at a place where such a sign is necessary, what it must feel like for this sign to be the first thing you see every morning when you drop your child off at school and the last thing you see at the end of the day. It seemed such a lame, sorry attempt at protecting these kids.

In the commotion surrounding the visit of the vice president's wife, no one else seemed to notice the sign, but once I'd read the words I couldn't concentrate on the event. Instead, I walked over to Joe Ehrman, the man who runs the program. Joe was once a football player with the Baltimore Colts, an NFL linebacker who'd gone into the ministry after retiring and then started this program to help kids.

I asked Joe what the neighborhood is like.

He shook his head and said, "One way during the day, another at night."

"Joe, what is up with that sign?" I asked.

"This is a tough neighborhood, Bill," he explained in a soft and patient voice. "These kids see everything. They see drugs, they see violence, and they see weapons. And if they see a gun, we want them to know what to do. As you can imagine, if Share Our Strength is here because these kids have hunger and nutrition issues, you can be sure they also have issues with access to housing, access to health care, and a whole range of needs that are all tied together."

We stood there looking out over these kids, who were just first, second, and third graders. They were at an age when school was still fun for them. They were sweet, mischievous perhaps, but still innocent. Yet as we stood staring at them, we knew that if we returned to their classroom in a mere six to eight years, many of these frolicking kids would be in serious, perhaps life-changing trouble. Some of the girls would be pregnant. Some of the boys would have joined gangs. Some, boys and girls alike, would have criminal records. It seemed impossible, looking at their six-year-old smiles, to believe that this would happen right before our eyes, or that we would let it happen. But statistics, past experience, and inadequate resources assured us that it would. One moment we can hold them in our arms, and the next they are slipping right between our fingers. Botanists watch plants grow using time-lapse photography. They can isolate the moment when a plant bends toward the light. They can freeze-frame, stop, and study it. But when is the moment a growing child bends toward darkness? And why must we wait to watch it on the eleven o'clock news?

What is the true condition of America's children today? Many are doing just fine, but fourteen million children still live below the poverty line, and millions of others are at risk from guns, lack of health care, and numerous other threats. Every day, 2,756 children drop out of high school, and 5,753 children are arrested. The essayist Roger Rosenblatt captured the hypocrisy that disguises our neglect in the title of an article he wrote for *The New York Times Magazine:* "The Society That Pretends to Love Children." In it, Marian Wright Edelman asks, "How do we honestly examine and transform the values and priorities of the wealthiest nation in history, which lets its children be the poorest group of Americans and lets a child get killed by guns every hour and a half? . . . How do we make it easier rather than harder for parents to balance work and family responsibilities and to get the community and financial support they need to carry out the most important task in America?"

It depends, of course, on who you ask. The Carnegie report will quantify how many children are at risk, but other foundations will brag about the opportunities that are unique to American children and that don't exist anywhere else in the world. Neither is wrong, but maybe we're asking the wrong question. Maybe the question is not, What is the true condition of America's children today?, but, rather, What should be the experience of all American children?

Hard times test the character of a nation, but in a different way, so do good times. These are indeed good times, and our blessings are not to be denied. The federal budget is in surplus, and state governments also enjoy extra resources. Wealth is being created at unprecedented levels in America, yet more of our children are in need than ever before. This is the paradox of America at the turn of the century. This is the challenge of our generation.

History's defining moments are often born of crisis. But the unlikely genesis of today's defining moment is an economic boom. Unemployment is at a twenty-four-year low. Inflation barely exists. The stock market roars. America is at peace. If this is not the set of conditions under which our nation can and should mount a successful campaign to save the next generation of at-risk children, then I don't know what is.

IV

Walker Percy once said that passing life's lessons on to our children is like two prisoners pushing notes between cell blocks. You can never tell if you are getting through, but you keep doing it anyhow.

Of course, our children have much to teach us as well.

Zach is a gifted and graceful athlete. Hockey is his passion, but he seems to have a natural ability in almost every sport. Seeing him field ground balls across our front yard fills me with wonder. He is fluid and natural. Watching him move is like watching a stream flow or a thoroughbred run, but it was not always this way.

Zach must benefit from a strong recessive gene somewhere in his DNA strand, because I can assure you he does not get his ability from me. I was so uncoordinated as a child that I fell going upstairs as well as down. I was so perpetually black-and-blue that my father called me Willy Lump-Lump. I shied away from team sports or stood in the outfield praying the ball would be hit anywhere but to me. I would rather have gone to the doctor for a penicillin shot than have Barry Belansky drill a pass at me that was certain to bounce off my chest and knock me over at the same time.

Still, baseball was a backdrop of my childhood. The high school field was dirt mixed with tar, and two blocks away. We preferred whatever part of the street in front of our house had no cars parked on it. Summer afternoons we'd play whiffle ball or throw a rubber ball off a set of terrace steps. If it bounced into the street it was a single, all the way across was a double, and if it reached the far lawn, it was a homer.

Only one thing besides darkness stopped our play: when the ball rolled down that sewer in front of the Monaghans' house. To this day, it is still almost impossible to think of that sewer as an inanimate object. It was a lifelong adversary to be outwitted, defeated, or forced into submission. It had taken too many balls to be forgiven or excused as an innocent party. There were days back then when the entire neighborhood could produce only one ball between everyone. If the sewer swallowed it, there was no running home to get another one. When it was gone, so was our ball game for that day.

Some days retrieving the ball became an activity in itself, one that kept us occupied far longer than any ball-game would. We would devise strategies that ranged from lowering the skinniest among us down into the sewer head first to helping the strongest pry off the heavy concrete manhole cover. Necessary equipment was commandeered from the neighborhood: rakes, brooms, tire irons. Sometimes night would come while we were still on our hands and knees, pointing flashlights and jiggling a long, twisted chain of wire shirt hangers, trying to coax the ball closer to our reach.

Those were summer days. Summer nights my father would come out onto the street after dinner in his khakis and white T-shirt to toss fly balls to a gaggle of boys. He'd throw the ball impossibly high, my first conclusive proof that he was no mere mortal. Each throw was like a firework launched, wriggling higher in its arc than the last and growing smaller at its peak. For a fraction of a moment, the ball would freeze and just hang there before dropping toward the five or six voices beneath it hollering over one another, "Mine, mine, I got it, mine!" The later and darker it got, the harder the ball was to catch and the more fun it seemed. When I think back on the many nights that finally ended with Dad piling all of the boys into his Chevy Impala to buy ice cream or pizza, I realize that it was mostly to give his arm a rest.

So teaching Zach to catch seemed an important and necessary paternal responsibility, right up there with teaching him to drive (someday). I started tossing a ball to Zach when he was four. "Spring training," I'd yell, and we'd dash through the garage, squeezing past the cars to grab our mitts from a shelf crowded with garden tools and buckets.

He would stand at one end of our sloped driveway in his short pants, pudgy as unshaped clay, betraying no hint of the long, lean figure he would develop even before his teens. He wore his baseball cap backward then and has neither taken it off nor turned it around since.

For about six weeks, it looked hopeless. Tossing a ball with a four-year-old is like having an overseas phone conversation. There is a disorienting two-second delay in the response. At first, Zach would raise his mitt to catch the ball just a moment after it had already bounced off his head or chest. After dropping the ball five or six times in a row (or was it fifty or sixty?), Zach would throw down the glove in anger, tears, or both. He'd let his body flop like a marionette cut loose from its strings. Defeat travels with plenty of excuses: "It's too hot," or "I'm thirsty." And, of course, "This glove is no good."

"That was my fault," I'd propose. "Those were bad throws. Let's try it again."

Once boredom set in, time was my enemy. I'd move closer and closer, trying to make it as easy as possible, tossing it softly, tossing it underhand. I explained how he needed to slap his other hand over the ball to keep it in his mitt. I explained how you couldn't look away, even for a second. I explained about watching the ball and not me. Finally, I stood so close, all but toe-to-toe with him, that I would not throw the ball but rather aim it for the dead center of his small orange mitt and drop it in. The first few times, Zach looked down at the ball in his glove with a mixture of surprise and skepticism, as if it were a candy bar that had dropped from a machine he hadn't put a coin into. I could see he was unsure whether it was he or I who had prevailed, but innocence reasserted itself and he assumed it must have been him. A smile broke out slowly across his face.

I can't tell you how many more times I put the ball in his glove before taking that first step back, and then a few steps more, before actually throwing it. I can't count that high. But gradually, like ice, his frustration melted away, and drop by drop his confidence increased. "Way to go! Wow, how did you ever catch *that* one." That confidence gave him the patience to keep learning and practicing. And the practice ultimately gave him something to be genuinely confident about.

Every year since that summer we've spent a good four or five months, from spring to fall, on the street in front of our house, tossing a ball back and forth. Sport for him, therapy for me. Everything from grounders to pop flies, or me down in a catcher's crouch, signaling for a fastball low and inside. After all this time it feels effortless, second nature. We could do it with our eyes closed. We talk or not. The *thwap* of a perfect pitch hitting the sweet spot of the mitt is often the only sound we need to hear.

I always try to remind myself that if it takes as long as it does to learn how to catch a ball, it must take a lot longer to learn the really important things in life. Algebra is harder than playing catch, as is understanding right from wrong, sharing, telling the truth, and learning how to live outside of oneself. A child's development demands we place the ball in his or her mitt over and over again. With the patience and commitment of the cathedral builders who laid brick on infinite brick, we must repeat, repeat, reinforce, and repeat again. We can't expect to be finished after the first time. The lessons need to be repeated, the rituals run through again, the stories retold.

Through baseball, hockey, and swim team—not to mention violin lessons and, later, drums—Zach learned more than skills and sports and techniques. He learned how to accept instruction, how to receive encouragement, and how to integrate criticism. It is equivalent to the cathedral builders' cornerstone, the foundation upon which all else depends and the one thing that he'll retain even after that unthinkably far-off time when his athletic skills diminish.

In *War and Peace,* General Kutuzov counsels that all battles are won through "time and patience, patience and time." They are different sides of the same coin, and when it comes to raising children, this indeed is the coin of the realm.

On a sunny spring morning, very early, in Mollie's room at the back of our house, her shade was pulled tight and her worn panda blanket was draped half across her like a toga. When I knelt to brush the hair from her face and gently squeeze her shoulder, her eyes fluttered open. I didn't give her a moment to complain.

"Mollie," I whispered in a conspiratorial voice whose promise she has grown to recognize, "you know what I think we should do?"

"What?" she asked, surprised and confused.

"Let's ride our bike around the neighborhood in our pajamas before anyone wakes up."

"Oh, Dad, can we please?"

We went to the garage and backed my bicycle onto our driveway. I snapped on Mollie's Styrofoam helmet and fastened her into the bike seat. Then we were off. The breeze caught Mollie's Little Mermaid nightgown, and its green fabric floated out behind her, with Flutter and Scuttle aloft just as Disney's animators dreamed it.

Mollie's hands, small and soft as cotton balls, squeezed my hips, and I wished I could fasten them there. She has never been the snuggler her older brother Zach is, which made this moment special for us in different ways. We hit a bump, and her grip tightened as she tucked chin and cheek between my shoulder blades. She was quiet, but I felt her head turning from side to side to take it all in. When she began to talk, the words came in a rush: "Dad, didya see . . . Dad, whatcha call . . . Dad, when can we . . ."

My "pajamas" were the gym shorts and T-shirt I slept in, but that didn't diminish Mollie's sense that we were engaged in something remarkable.

"Mom's not gonna believe this, is she, Dad? Let me tell her when she wakes up, okay? Don't say anything. And let's not even tell Zach at all," she implored, with a child's intuition that magic revealed will be magic ruined.

Two summers have passed since that morning, but Mollie remembers it clearly. So do I, mostly because we had so much fun. It also reinforced that being successful with children is like being successful onstage. It takes more than just reading a script as written; it requires breathing life into it, transforming stage directions into compelling art.

V

We've been treating successive generations of at-risk children too narrowly, as a challenge for social science or medical science, when what we really need to do is create a new art form. This became clear spending a morning with Dr. Debra Frank, founder of Boston City Hospital's Failure to Thrive Clinic.

In a presidential campaign, it's called the war room. In the White House, it's called the situation room. At Boston City Hospital's Failure to Thrive Clinic, the doctors are too busy and too humble to call it anything other than what it is: a coatroom. This is where they meet as a team every Wednesday to review cases and weigh and choose strategies. There are no maps, computers, or telephone hot lines, just file folders on a long brown table and the empathy of eight specialists who spend their days in the neighborhoods and homes of Boston's poorest families. This room is where they puzzle together why babies born into the city's poorest families are not gaining weight and growing as they should and what must be done to save their lives.

Poverty's paradox is that it creates medical problems that can't be cured with medicine, so these doctors find themselves looking for vital signs that can't be found with a stethoscope: in household budgets, parent-child dynamics, and family histories. In their search for cures they seek to mobilize a wide array of community resources, not just medical resources.

This means Dr. Frank must be more than the combination pediatrician, researcher, advocate, and social worker that she is. She must be a first-rate fund-raiser as well. It is not uncommon for her to begin a conversation by asking, with the directness of a drug kingpin demanding to know whether you've brought the unmarked bills, "Are you going to give us the money?" It is the same tone of voice she uses before congressional committees in Washington, where her testimony about pediatric health care is sought and respected for the reliable scientific evidence upon which it is based. If she talks fast and dispenses with pleasantries, it's because she has a clear line of sight to the lives of babies who will literally be saved because of her team's work, and she is in a big hurry to reach them.

During the morning, I sat in as an observer. Those present—doctors, social workers, home visitors—were careful to use only the first names of patients to protect their confidentiality. We crowded around a table on lopsided swivel chairs and folding chairs, the walls behind us hung with shelves for coats, shoes, and faded secondhand clothing that, along with food from the makeshift pantry next door, supplements the medical needs of patients.

Everyone in the room looked worn down by the now familiar pattern of these meetings. Dr. Frank was at one end of the table, wearing a white lab coat over a floral-print dress that seemed defiant of the season. She sighed and flipped patients' charts onto the table, calling out names and asking for updates. These young patients are vulnerable and dependent. The situations their families are in don't make it easy to help. One mom had no phone. One mom couldn't be found. Another family's divorce had put treatment on hold.

There are many questions about the home of each child, but not enough answers. The clinic's staff seems less frustrated than resigned. With a caseload of more than 170 low-income families, the challenge is daunting. Some of the cases circle the room like dishwater around the drain, then swirl beyond the team's grasp, their places taken by new stories of hardship that cascade down upon this beleaguered staff. I expect the cynicism or pessimism of veteran cops taking a stolen-car report, but find instead a weary steadfastness on behalf of every child discussed.

Toward the end of the meeting, one case had everyone stumped. A twenty-six-month-old boy had not gained an ounce in four months. His physical and mental development, future health, and capacity for learning were at serious risk. His mom was single and poor, and the house where he lived suffered from what one home visitor called "a high level of disorganization," a euphemism for a mom who is not there enough. But the mother insisted there was always enough food for her children, and this was what baffled everyone.

The boy's growth chart was scrutinized, put down, and picked up again. Those familiar with the child offered whatever information they had, but none of it seemed to yield any answers.

"You're sure that the mom is keeping enough food on hand?"

"That's the mystery."

Finally, Dr. Frank asked, "Is there a high chair in the house?"

For just a moment, everyone paused.

"No," replied the home visitor.

Everyone around the table shook their heads knowingly.

"The child is fed on the floor or in his walker."

This family had food. What it lacked was other necessary resources and perhaps a parent with sufficient skills to deploy them.

As Dr. Frank told me: "Malnutrition is not just a medical condition, but a social and economic condition as well. Historically, childhood malnutrition has not been identified properly and has been addressed with a purely medical model, which is often ineffective." The medical approach alone is too narrow, so Boston City Hospital provides for a multitude of both clinical and social needs. Families are provided not only with food and nutritional supplements, but also with transportation to the clinic, referral to other government services, legal aid, and outreach services to their homes. Families are provided with donated clothing and supermarket vouchers solicited from private donors. Boston City Hospital also maintains close ties with home-less shelters, WIC sites, treatment programs for drug-abusing mothers, day-care programs, Head Start, and other community services.

Huddled in this coatroom on the fifth floor, it felt as if something subversive or unsanctioned was taking place, as if the clinic's work were a form of avant-garde medicine, not widely practiced or sufficiently funded, but sustained by a unique vision that is only just beginning to resonate with a new generation of child health-care providers. Dr. Frank and her colleagues are redefining the role of doctor, dramatically expanding the catalog of things doctors care about, probe for, and prescribe. They are on the cutting edge of a new social philosophy that treats the challenge of rescuing sick children from the ravages of poverty as more of an art than a science. As avant-garde artists, they have not been afraid to reject the rigid doctrines of the past and boldly add new colors to their palette, new shapes to their canvas.

Most important of all, it works. Eighty-five percent of the children treated at the clinic have had their malnutrition reversed and have assumed normal growth and development rates. Although those around the table constitute one of the elite teams in modern medicine today, throughout the course of the morning I never heard a single request for expensive tests or advanced medical technologies. Their strategy instead is to push beyond the limits of even the most sophisticated medical practices and scientific knowledge, until they've mastered the art of understanding how children and their families live their lives.

CHAPTER THREE

Coming Up Taller

I

Nancy Carstedt is the executive director of the Chicago Children's Choir, the largest choral and performance training group of its kind in the United States. As much as Nancy Carstedt loves music, that is not the focal point of her work. Her work is about saving children's lives. She succeeds at it by letting kids into a world they've never even imagined, exposing them to discipline and commitment and excellence—in this case, musical excellence—and by doing whatever is necessary to enable them to create and experience excellence themselves.

Forty public schools in Chicago channel more than three thousand inner-city children into the choir's three-part program. In addition to choral music education programs in schools, there are six neighborhood choirs and the world-renowned Concert Choir. It has performed everywhere from the White House to *The Oprah Winfrey Show,* with the Chicago Symphony Orchestra and the Joffrey Ballet, in South Africa, Russia, Italy, and Japan. The choir is multiracial and multicultural, and like any choir, harmony is its business.

Seventy-nine percent of the students in the Chicago school system come from low-income families. They know broken homes and dangerous streets. That is why many are trapped in Chicago's troubled public school system to begin with. Opportunity is something they've been taught to fight for, not expect. Nearly fifteen thousand teenagers drop out of that school system each year, about the same number that are entering the pre-K program at the other end.

For these kids, the choir is everything: their safe space, their caring adult, their form of family discipline, and their proof that hard work yields rewards. It is their ticket to places across the city and around the world where most of their classmates will never go. It is both saving and shaping their lives. Their signature red blazers, with the breast-pocket emblem of the choir, represent America's largest, most comprehensive organization devoted to the musical education of children, and for many members, the blazer represents a pride in themselves they have not known before.

In 1998, Carstedt phoned me to introduce herself and schedule a visit. She had an ambition and a vision for the choir unlike anything I'd heard before. She wanted the choir to reach more kids and to be able to support its future growth. She was frustrated that something that had proven so effective in supporting children was, with relatively modest expenses of about $1.2 million a year, almost fully dependent on grants and charitable handouts for its own survival, and therefore severely limited in its ability to grow. Instead of devoting her considerable drive and energy to creating new programs for the children and expanding her vision of what the choir could be, most of her hours were spent raising money, identifying budget savings, writing grant proposals, courting individual donors, struggling with operating deficits, and debating choices that shouldn't be necessary in the first place. She was determined to find another way.

Her instinct was that nonprofit organizations like the Chicago Children's Choir could become more self-sufficient and less dependent upon charitable donations. Her vision of how to achieve that went far beyond the job description of choir director. Nancy wanted to build the first youth performing arts center in the country. She wanted to build a commercial recording studio. She wanted marketing and licensing partnerships with global companies like British Airways and Evian to support the choir's international travel. Properly structured, the partnerships could benefit the companies as much as the choir. She believed revenues could be earned rather than begged, and was so certain of it that she convinced the Chicago Community Trust to underwrite a year's sabbatical, which she used to travel and meet with social entrepreneurs around the country in search of better ways to support the choir.

Over the phone, her bubbly enthusiasm was conveyed in

a voice that was high and excited, with a scratchy quality that disguised granite determination. She made an appointment to meet with me and several colleagues. That's where I would learn that there was even more to Nancy Carstedt than met the eye, that she had reached a destination in life as unlikely as could be, given where she'd started. The turning point in Carstedt's journey was a catastrophic event. She knew what it meant to be lifted, literally, from the ground and cared for until well.

Nancy Carstedt was not what I expected. Dressed in a conservative tweed suit and an elegant string of pearls, close to sixty years old, she looked better suited to organizing a garden or bridge club than thousands of at-risk youth drawn from Chicago's unforgiving streets. So short that in a crowd of choir members she wouldn't reach even the shoulders of most of them, her compact frame nevertheless suggested an immovable object that would prevail over an irresistible force.

For two hours, we talked about her vision for the choir, its growth and independence. Her pride and enthusiasm for the quality of its members' artistic achievement was as authentic as the CDs she brought of their best performances around the world. Since she'd been with the choir for seven years, I wondered about her career prior to that, wondered what experience her work was built upon and what she had done with her first fifty years. There was something unusual about the path she'd taken, and while I couldn't tell what it was, it nagged at me. Near the end of our conversation, I couldn't resist asking in a casual, genuinely curious tone: "Nancy, what were you doing before the choir?" I could never have guessed the answer.

"I worked at an exterminating company," she replied looking me in the eye, and then looking away for just a moment.

I feared I was being naive, that "exterminating company" was a new term of art in the business world, like "junk bond" or "venture capital," that was now being applied to the nonprofit world. I nodded my head by rocking my whole body forward. "Uh-huh." There was a long pause. Finally she elaborated: She worked for a real exterminating company, the kind that got rid of pests. What else could you say to that?

"You know, I feel like I can tell you about it because I've read what you wrote about your mother's depression," she said, referring to the chapter I'd written about my family in *Revolution of the Heart,* a book about Share Our Strength's work. "I've had some experience with depression myself," she explained, as she quietly told more about herself.

Nancy first encountered depression following the birth of her daughter. She didn't seek relief through therapy until later, when the depression intensified after the death of her mother in 1972. Following that, her eighteen-year marriage dissolved, along with a storybook suburban lifestyle that included her work as a speech pathologist and a variety of volunteer activities on behalf of kids.

Any divorce brings pain to a family, but the consequences for the Carstedts were almost unimaginable. Nancy's depression deepened. Her body wasted to just seventy-two pounds. The breakup was more than her adopted son Blaine could bear. At fifteen, he attempted suicide, but succeeded only in leaving himself a quadriplegic for life. Nancy devoted herself full-time to his care. What happened next was as predictable as it was tragic. "I grew even more depressed. I started to drink and eventually developed such a serious problem with alcoholism that I fell down drunk in a Chicago gutter. Someone picked me up and put me in a hospital, where I began a very long road back to recovery. It included a five-month stay at Hazelden in Minnesota for chemical dependency treatment and a fifteen-month stay in Highland Park Hospital's psychiatric ward for treatment of depression."

Depression is a soft and sanitized word. It's the wrong word. It implies that something or somebody has been pushed down, that there was a yielding rather than a shattering. It's still thought of more as a condition than the grave, debilitating injury its victims experience. There's got to be another word for what Nancy went through, and another word still for going through it so long that the seasons outside your window cycle around a second time. Recovering from depression should qualify you for the Navy SEALs team or the Army's Green Berets. There's very little else that you won't be able to do.

Most of the time, Nancy was in a psychiatric ward. There was a suicide attempt. When she got out of the hospital in 1986, she was burdened with the second mortgage she'd taken out on her home and thirty thousand dollars' of credit-card debt that had been used to finance health-care and child-care expenses. Unsure of her own capacity for joining the workforce, she took a secretarial position with an exterminating company.

About three years later, a sorority sister who knew of Nancy's struggle reintroduced her to a former Northwestern University classmate who worked at the Chicago Community Trust. He knew that the Chicago Children's Choir was looking for an executive director and encouraged her to apply. "The what?" she responded. "I'd never heard of the choir."

The choir's board was impressed with her history of volunteer activities, ranging from work at a community nursery school to crisis intervention for teens. They offered her the job, and it has been her consuming passion ever since.

As any recovering alcoholic or victim of depression knows, there is no final triumph over either, just a constant inner vigilance that takes its own quiet toll. But it is also a source of strength, what Carter Echols, a minister at Washington National Cathedral, calls "the almost always forgotten power of our brokenness." It gave Nancy certain advantages. People matter to her. Healing matters. She not only found her way out of the darkness, she found a way to make it count. She is governed as much by her heart as by her head, a quality sneered at in certain business circles but essential for building anything that even resembles a cathedral. "Obviously, I'm not black, and I've never really been poor," Nancy told me, adding with characteristic understatement, "but I feel like I know these kids."

II

Nancy Carstedt's seven years at the Chicago Children's Choir have been more about the kids than the music. The choir is an unlikely combination of north- and south-siders who listen to rap and rock and roll, but sing with the city's symphony from a repertoire that ranges from Bach and Handel to Mozart and Brahms. They perform up to one hundred concerts a year and have toured not only the United States but South Africa, Russia, Italy, and Japan. "Children must have a place where they can grow together," she explains, "where they can feel safe from the danger of the streets, where they can build healthy relationships with caring adults, and most important, where they can succeed."

The choir has accomplished social objectives that policy-makers would never have dreamed. One alumnus remembers, "I spent about a third of my childhood—from 1963 to 1969—as a member of the Chicago Children's Choir. At a time when true integration was a radical idea, I was part of a multiracial, multicultural, and extremely talented group of young people who shared something special with Chicago and the world. We were given the gift of voice at birth. Through our song and our friendship with each other, we shared the gift of balance, harmony, and music. Graham Greene once wrote, 'There is always one moment in childhood when the door opens and lets the future in.' The choir is the doorway. . . ." One hundred percent of the choir's graduating seniors in 1995 have gone on to higher education.

Carstedt can give you a thousand examples of the choir's long-lasting impact on the lives of the children, but she really needs only one. "It was my first year, 1990, and one of the choir alumni who had been very popular was in the hospital dying of AIDS. I'll never forget it. He was only twenty-seven. I didn't really know him well, but everyone was pressing me to go and visit and to pay my respects to the family on behalf of the choir, because the choir had been a huge part of his life. So I went. His name was David. He was in a coma. At first, I just stood at the door and looked into the room, stunned, unsure of what to do. I was completely shocked at what the disease could do, at the shrunken, shriveled form beneath the hospital bedsheets. I went in and spent a few minutes by his bedside. Finally, just as I was about to leave, I looked up and saw it. His red choir jacket from ten years before was pinned up above the head of his bed, and the window ledges were filled with jacket covers from recordings he had made with the choir."

Nancy Carstedt's experience with the choir has been a special one, but it is not uncommon. All of us have seen programs in our communities—from choirs to youth hockey, from remedial reading to mentoring—that turn kids in a positive direction and keep them there. The scope and breadth of what they cover is breathtaking. One small foundation in New York that I've had the privilege to chair, the Echoing Green Foundation, funds young social entrepreneurs as far upstream as possible and has, by itself, supported and helped launch organizations that address education reform, community service, women's issues, prison reform, and many other social problems.

There are three facts about programs like the choir and others described above that are virtually indisputable. The first is that there are tens of thousands of such programs around the country. They are designed to support children and teens. They are community-based, locally supported, and operate essentially alone and independently from each other. Most were created by a charismatic leader who had some personal experience with or exposure to the problem that he or she is attempting to solve. The late Reverend Christopher Moore founded the Chicago Children's Choir in 1956 at Hyde Park's First Unitarian Church.

The second demonstrable fact is that, across the country, the quality of these organizations is very uneven. Some have highly trained professional staffs, others rely on volunteers, but there are many that make a concrete difference in the lives of kids, adding skills, support, and value to them in ways that will improve their lives forever. Increasingly, such programs fill a gap left by government cutbacks that no other entity has filled.

But third, and tragically, those programs that work and those that don't work meet the same fate: They are underfunded, unreplicated, and in some cases essentially unnoticed. Even the very best ones do not get to scale, do not reach more than a fraction of those who need their services, and often do not endure. Under the backward logic of this Alice in Wonderland world, success does not guarantee success. It certainly doesn't guarantee survival. It is not a predictor of additional support beyond a certain level. Given what is at stake—a generation of children crying out for our help—some new form of ingenuity must be applied to redress such an unconscionable situation. It would simply not be tolerated under most other circumstances.

For example, imagine if, after years of research and clinical trials, a physician at University Hospital in Chicago achieved a long-sought breakthrough and developed a protocol to successfully treat breast cancer or colon cancer. Imagine having the tools to eradicate both the disease and the suffering. It's unthinkable that the treatment would be confined only to the patients of that one hospital. It's equally unthinkable that many years and thousands of cured patients later the successful treatment would be abandoned because the doctor who discovered it changed jobs or retired, or because the hospital failed to raise enough money to keep using it.

If anything, the opposite would occur. Doctors from around the world would do whatever was necessary to come to Chicago and learn the appropriate procedures. Medical journals would document the research and resulting therapy with great precision. Venture capitalists would invest in the biotech firms or pharmaceutical companies that produced the drugs enabling them, in turn, to accelerate other research. Consumer demand, expressed through patients and their families, would make itself felt. The necessary mechanisms would be in place to respond to it. With an effective remedy finally at hand, every effort would be made to ensure its widespread availability and affordability.

What if a different kind of cancer has finally surrendered to aggressive treatment? Think of the cancer of gangs, drugs, and violence that destroys the connective tissue of our cities and the suffering it creates. Think of the cancer of racism and ignorance that suppresses opportunity and destroys the cells that carry hope to the heart. For more than three thousand kids under the expert care of the Chicago Children's Choir, this cancer is in remission. The mortality rate hasn't been reduced to zero with medicine that can never be guaranteed, but both quality of life and the odds of longevity have certainly been improved.

Choirs alone are not the panacea to our social problems, but they do create favorable outcomes that we can predict and replicate—if we understand how, and if we have the will.

Now consider the analogy described above, but played out across the entire country. Imagine that Pittsburgh's Children's Hospital can cure cystic fibrosis, Rose Hospital in Denver can treat respiratory disease, the Houston Medical Center finds a cure for diabetes, and Johns Hopkins Hospital knows how to reverse hypertension. Each of these institutions can do one thing well, but none of them can do more than that. Unfortunately, in this imagined world, even the most remarkable advances in health care would be of little use to most patients, who typically present with multiple conditions. If anything, they enjoy a false hope but ultimately succumb, unnecessarily, to an illness whose cure has already been discovered somewhere else, somewhere unavailable to them.

Social analyst and Harvard lecturer Lisbeth Schorr, in her book *Common Purpose,* examined thousands of models of excellent schools, effective job training, youth development, and antipoverty programs and concluded that "we have learned to create the small exceptions that can change the lives of hundreds. But we have not learned how to make the exceptions the rule to change the lives of millions." She expressed the hope that "leaders, national and local, will emerge to convey to the American public a new understanding not only about the depth of our disarray and the disaster it portends, but also about the remarkable accomplishments we are now capable of because we have so much of the knowledge we need."

The one thing more tragic than an incurable disease is knowing effective treatment and withholding it or failing to ensure its widespread use. That is what is happening in America today. It is the most persistent condition impeding true social reform. The greatest obstacle is not money, it is the lack of genuine understanding of or appreciation for programs that work in a world that has changed. We don't need new cures to be invented or old ones to be reinvented. Medical science does not waste resources by continuing to research a polio vaccine when we've long had a very good one. The challenge instead is to take what works and ensure its wider availability.

That's the challenge that fuels Nancy Carstedt's quest and sustains her hope for the children of Chicago.

III

In November 1998, I saw the Chicago Children's Choir perform at the annual fund-raising dinner they call Red Jacket Optional. This is what the word "harmony" was invented to connote. In their red blazers, ranging in age from eleven to seventeen, these children—and the voice of song that emerged from such diversity of black, white, Hispanic, and Asian—were pleasure and sermon combined. The boys choir. The show choir. Soloists. Ensembles. The full choir. Their performances were interspersed throughout the evening. I won't try to re-create the experience. The arrangement of words on paper is no match for the arrangement and voices of 120 kids on risers. Early in the evening, waiting for the elevator in the lobby of the Chicago Cultural Center, you could hear them rehearsing up on the fifth floor. A stranger waiting with me turned and said softly: "They sound like angels, don't they?"

It was the third time in three weeks that I'd been with Nancy Carstedt, following a board retreat earlier in the month and a conference we'd attended in Colorado Springs along with two hundred other social entrepreneurs. It had been interesting to see her in different settings, playing different roles with board, staff, children, and supporters.

The choir is a forty-three-year-old organization. Nancy made it her mission to take it in new directions. She's advocated everything from creating a revenue-generating choir school to starting a bus company (because lack of transportation is one of the greatest obstacles for children hoping to participate in after-school activities).

It hasn't always been easy. It's been said that no one likes change except a wet baby. Like any active board would, the choir's board vigorously debated Nancy's new ideas. Her staff at times has had more immediate short-term needs on which they'd prefer to focus, so this has also been an opportunity to watch her adjust to the challenges of leadership.

Usually, Nancy sets herself apart slightly from her colleagues at the choir. I often see her sitting alone, usually working, reviewing donor lists, making notes. Impatient with resistance but cognizant of the need to build support for each step she takes, she leads from a position of strength, with a reservoir of respect to draw upon. Her investment in the choir has been so substantial, her commitment so total, that others defer to her as they would to a majority stockholder who everyone acknowledges has the right to call the shots.

Much like a cathedral builder, her vision of the work has been expansive. The Chicago Children's Choir is not just an arts organization any more than a cathedral is just a building. To Nancy, it is every bit as much about youth development. It is about changing and saving lives. I listened recently as she tried to explain this to a banker whose foundation could give the choir a needed financial boost. Nancy shared the comments of the director of a youth theater program, who said: "There is no way to fast-forward and know how the kids will look back on this, but I have seen the joy in their eyes and have heard it in their voices, and I have watched them take a bow and come up taller."

"Coming up taller." Both image and phrase succeed, don't they? President Clinton's Committee on the Arts and the Humanities liked it so much that they used it as the title of their report to the nation on how arts organizations like the Chicago Children's Choir provide critical developmental tools for children. Choirs fit the Carnegie Council on Adolescent Development's definition of what at-risk kids need most: "They must have sustained, caring relationships with adults; receive guidance in facing serious challenges; become valued members of a constructive peer group; feel a sense of worth as a person; become socially competent; . . . find expression of the curiosity and exploration that strongly characterizes their age; believe in a promising future with real opportunities; and find ways of being useful to others."

The fund-raising dinner was a great success. With one exception, all eyes were on the choir as it performed throughout the evening. The exception was Nancy Carstedt. She turned to watch the expressions of the parents and donors instead. She scanned the audience to see if they were feeling what she was feeling. Like an appraiser of fine art, she sought to confirm her assessment of the market value of her holdings. What she said in a whisper when she turned to me was almost redundant, given how clearly I could read it in her face. "Boy, if we can't turn this into something, we're in the wrong business."

"If only there were more Nancy Carstedts," a foundation president said to me wistfully at a recent conference. It's a tempting thought. Our society certainly needs their leadership, innovation, and courage. Foundations want to find such people and invest in them early, but no one is sure how to do it. Are they born, or can they also be made? What leads somebody to suddenly change their life and devote themselves to others? Are effective community leaders a product of luck, or can we sow and nurture the seeds that yield them? One man who has devoted a good part of his life trying to find out is Gregg Petersmeyer.

Petersmeyer was a top aide to President George Bush and was instrumental in the Bush administration's volunteerism initiatives and the founding of The Points of Light Foundation. After a career in consulting, venture capital, and then government, Petersmeyer decided that the potential of effective action at the grassroots level seemed to hold the most promise. A devoted father of three, now in his early fifties, Petersmeyer is a man who sees the goodness in others and has thought deeply about how to release it.

After he left the White House, Petersmeyer traveled the country meeting with thousands of community leaders to identify and better understand the ingredients of their success, and particularly of their transformation from concerned citizens to committed activists. He wanted to know why one man who lives next to a proposed toxic-waste site goes to work every day and minds his business while another quits his job to stop the site's construction and create a neighborhood environmental organization. Why does one mother of three drive her kids to choir practice and another travel the country relentlessly to bring about a new understanding of how choirs affect young lives?

Through his research, a variety of factors contributing to community activism were identified, including one that Petersmeyer called "the random triggering event." For most activists, there was a catalytic, perhaps dramatic, occurrence that seemed to push them across the line from concerned to committed, from talk to action, from individual expression to organized and collective action. I could identify with this. I remember reading about the catastrophic Ethiopian famine in *The Washington Post* one morning and the impact it had on my decision to start Share Our Strength. For years I'd been troubled by hunger in America and around the world, mostly because its persistence seemed so cruel and unnecessary in the face of the abundance we enjoy. Yet just moments after reading the *Post* coverage, I was doing something about it; for some reason and for the first time I was urgently putting in place the pieces of a new organization that would change and consume my life for more than two decades.

As a former consultant at McKinsey & Company, known for its analytic methodologies and deductive reasoning, Petersmeyer had been trained to figure out the important questions to ask about phenomena such as random triggering events. The important question he came up with was: How do you make such triggering events nonrandom? If you could make them nonrandom—that is, if you could prescribe and predict the conditions that create them—you could better ensure the desired outcome of more people engaged in their community, and not just leave such matters to chance.

Petersmeyer's work in this area is still ongoing, now from his position as one of the senior staff and board members of America's Promise–The Alliance for Youth, the organization that General Colin Powell started to marshal more resources for children. The question he's pursuing is a fascinating one, and its pursuit reveals that the triggering factor is not an external event so much as an internal event. It's not about something you see happen in the world but rather about a strength you see inside yourself. The catalytic event is not learning something new about a problem like hunger, but learning something new about your own unique ability to contribute to its solution.

By the time I finished reading about the Ethiopian famine, I knew no more about how to solve such a problem than I did before I started, but I read it at a time in my life when I'd just finished learning a lot more about myself. The presidential campaign of Senator Gary Hart, with whom I'd worked for a decade, had come to an end. In the course of it, I'd learned about community organizing, fund-raising, public relations, and recruiting volunteers. The skills necessary for starting Share Our Strength were the ones I'd just acquired. The organization's creation was less a reaction to a triggering event—important as the Ethiopian famine was to my thinking—than it was an unlocking and unleashing of emotion and skills. As it is for the children who take a bow and come up taller upon knowing the power of self-expression, finding and under-standing one's strengths, a necessary prelude to sharing them, is a profoundly empowering experience.

We have a long way to go before we can clone more Nancy Carstedts. Personal motivation is rich and varied and often mysterious. There will always be a variety of fac-tors like charisma, confidence, availability of resources, and unforeseen circumstances that energize and persuade people to take actions they might not even have known they were capable of. There will always be random trig-gering events that anger, inspire, or provide individuals with the opportunity for deeper reflection.

If there is a role to be played in making these triggering events less random, it is in showing people where to look, in turning their direction inward rather than outward, in helping them see the strengths within. It's what Vaclav Havel, playwright and president of Czechoslovakia, under-stood when he came to the United States in 1990 and told a joint session of the U.S. Congress that "the salvation of this human world lies nowhere else than in the human heart, in the human power to reflect, in human meekness, and in human responsibility."

CHAPTER FOUR

The Battle Between
Idealism and Cynicism

I

"Alan willed this" was the common refrain in Cleveland on a Wednesday afternoon in June 1998.

"It was pure force of will on Alan's part."

"He's worked on this nonstop for more than four years. The president had no choice."

"Alan made the president come to Cleveland."

Many similar comments could be heard that day about City Year cofounder Alan Khazei, as Secret Service agents quietly assumed positions throughout the gym at John Carroll University, anticipating the arrival of the motorcade of the president of the United States.

Cleveland was host to CYZYGY, the annual conference of about one thousand City Year staff and corps members from the ten cities they serve. City Year says its mission is "to tap the civic power of youth for an annual campaign of idealism," which it does by creating opportunities for community service. In a typical year, corps members dedicate more than 275,000 hours to tutoring at-risk children, aid more than 17,000 people in disaster relief efforts, and refurbish almost 1,000 schools and community centers. They serve as teacher assistants and violence prevention instructors, and they promote HIV/AIDS awareness. They build urban gardens.

Corps members work in corporate-sponsored teams. They begin each morning with a regimen of calisthenics, wearing distinctive red, black, and khaki uniforms. Ranging in age from seventeen to twenty-three, they reflect a rich diversity of ethnic, socioeconomic, and educational backgrounds. There is not another organization in the country where you will find such large numbers of black, white, Latino, and Asian young people working so closely together. What City Year demonstrates in achieving racial healing and tolerance will far outlast any playgrounds its corps members build or parks they clean.

The president's trip to Cleveland was not the only thing Alan Khazei has willed. I've known Alan for more than fifteen years, since he was a twenty-year-old campaign organizer responsible for the town of Nashua, New Hampshire, in Gary Hart's 1984 presidential primary campaign. Hart had the least amount of money and the lowest initial name recognition in a crowded field. Nevertheless, Hart won Nashua, as he did the state, in an upset victory that led the network news and put him on the cover of every national newsmagazine.

"Two weeks after I joined the campaign staff," Khazei

recalls, "*Newsweek* magazine predicted that Hart would be the first candidate to leave the race due to problems raising money and support. Nonetheless, eight months later, Gary Hart won the New Hampshire primary with a comfortable margin and scored a stunning upset over the acknowledged front-runners in the race, Vice President Mondale and Senator John Glenn. It was the New Hampshire victory that gave me the confidence to start City Year," Khazei admits today. "It showed that anything was possible. I realized that even without a lot of money or visible support, a small group of committed people and a powerful idea could lead to big change."

In May 1987, when Hart withdrew from his second presidential campaign because of the press uproar over his personal life, he later shocked the country by dramatically reentering the race in December on the steps of the New Hampshire statehouse. A lengthy and passionate memo from Alan Khazei urging—practically insisting—on just such a course was no small factor in his decision to do so.

A decade ago, Alan Khazei graduated from Harvard Law School. If you asked him then what he planned to do, he answered the same way he answers now: "Change the world." He says it with a warm, welcoming smile stretched over steely determination. It is a smile that says, "I'll be your friend even if you think what I'm trying to do is ridiculous." Alan does not give up easily; he is to persistence what Starbucks is to coffee. It didn't seem possible to him that the president of the United States could not come to speak to City Year in Cleveland.

Michael Brown was cofounder of City Year with Alan and probably knows him better than anyone. "I met Alan the first day of freshman year at Harvard. We were assigned to be roommates. My first impression of Alan was that he was a little too enthusiastic about everything; I was still trying to be cool. He was ready to organize dances and school events from the word go. But soon I learned that his enthusiasm was not merely infectious, but he also had these remarkable qualities of analysis and sincere empathy for people. People would seek him out for advice, including me. He also had this complete faith that one person could make a difference. I remember one night he told me that if I really believed in John Anderson for president in 1980, then I could make a difference in his campaign. I ended up volunteering for John Anderson in the 1980 campaign."

Alan makes it sound as if fate had a hand in the creation of City Year:

Like many college students, the summer after my junior year I traveled to our nation's capital for an internship with my congressperson, Norman D'Amours, from my home state of New Hampshire. The main project of my internship was to prepare a report on the feasibility of a comprehensive national service program as an alternative to bringing back the draft.

That same summer, my college roommate, Michael Brown, was finishing up a "year off" from school, working as a legislative assistant to Congressperson Leon Panetta. Michael oversaw a bill that Congressman Panetta introduced to set up a national commission to study establishing a national service system for the United States. That bill was scheduled for congressional hearings that summer. Consequently, at just age twenty, we had the full services of the Library of Congress and resources of congressional offices to dive into our policy passion—the idea of national service. Although the specific idea for City Year did not get formed until several years later, in many ways our commitment to putting our energy to work to help bring about national service in America was sealed that summer.

But it was more than the Library of Congress and the external resources of congressional offices that fueled Khazei's passion. As he wrote for Harvard's Career Book last year:

During that summer I also attended a meeting of Ralph Nader with a group of interns. His words stayed with me long afterward. I had admired Ralph Nader for a long time as someone who, by fully occupying the office of citizen, had singlehandedly done so much to improve our society. Nader's message to us was something akin to:"It is during your twenties that your idealism will be at its highest point. You will also be your freest to pursue your ideals and the issues you are most passionate about, as you won't have the obligations of a new family, a home mortgage, or other material debts. You will not, as of yet, be broken down by a society that chips away at your idealism, encouraging you to compromise and be more 'practical' and 'realistic' as you get older. Consequently, I urge you to use this time in your twenties to take risks. Pursue your wildest dreams and ambitions. Do the unconventional, and try to make a difference in the world."

Several years later, when I ultimately decided to pursue City Year right out of law school, I still had the voice of Ralph Nader ringing in my ears.

Alan is one of three children born to an Iranian father and an Italian mother, a surgeon and a nurse, respectively, who met in the operating room one day and ultimately made their home in Kittaning, Pennsylvania. At Alan's wedding on Martha's Vineyard in 1997, his best man told how Alan's mother went with him to his school bus stop every day, all the way up through high school, and stood outside the window yelling, "I love you, Alan." Instead of being embarrassed, Alan wondered, Where are all of the other mothers? Alan told me that he saw City Year as "an institution designed to express my mother's love."

In the ten years following its founding, Alan devoted himself to City Year. Working out of an abandoned warehouse, the group began with a fifty-member corps in Boston, and eventually expanded to three hundred corps members, and then to nine other cities. Alan would fight for the national legislation that created President Clinton's AmeriCorps program and help shape it. He would position his own organization to reap more than $8 million a year in federal funding. But the road through the inner city, where

City Year works, is not an easy one. Early in its history, City Year saw a Boston corps member shot and killed. More recently, another in Chicago committed suicide. The at-risk youths who make up much of the corps need extensive support to succeed. Funds to grow the program are always scarce. Talent is in short supply. Alan's ambition for the organization could not be realized without assuming risks that scared many. There were times when both staff and board resisted. He never wavered.

I I

"All successful human endeavors—from breakthrough inventions like the telephone to great social leaps forward like the civil rights movement—begin with the assumption that change is possible. Cynicism is the enemy of positive change because it discourages creative thinking and destroys both the belief that change is possible and the will to act. The first step toward putting idealism to work is to reject cynicism and embrace idealism."

This is the first of more than 160 specific tips and techniques cataloged in the City Year handbook for putting idealism to work. It derives from a worldview that co-founders Alan Khazei and Michael Brown share. As Michael Brown explained to students at John Carroll University in 1994: "When I was in college—just a little over a decade ago—our entire society was still organized around one defining struggle: the struggle between capitalism and communism, between the United States and the Soviet Union. The Cold War shaped our economy, our educational priorities, certainly our military priorities—and perhaps most of all, our sense of what was possible. . . . Today, the Cold War has given way to a new battle, the battle between idealism and cynicism, which will be the defining struggle of our society for years to come."

Brown believes that the most effective way to defeat cynicism is through national service. He can envision a time when instead of college students being asked "What do you plan to do after you graduate?" the question will be "How are you going to spend your service year?"

> *Imagine that young people unite from all backgrounds and experiences: African Americans, Asian Americans, Caucasians, Latinos, kids from the suburbs, kids from the cities. They run an after-school program, a neighborhood recycling program, they build a community playground, they tutor and mentor inner-city school students. . . . This is the extraordinary promise of voluntary national service. . . . It would be a catalyst for the common good. It would help the country move forward—breaking through apathy, disaffection, misunderstanding, and special interest. It would shatter social barriers by uniting rich and poor, and black and white— Simi Valley and South Central Los Angeles. Long-term, it could help make our democracy more responsive, more effective, more thoughtful, and more just.*

One of the things that makes City Year unique is an obsessive insistence on infusing everything with meaning, which has led to the development of a strong organizational culture. Mike Brown recalls when their dilapidated first headquarters was burglarized, and an alarm company came to put in an alarm. "When the guy finished installing it, he asked us to come up with a five-digit code to get in, and we decided it would be 19682, which meant that in 1968 the country lost both Dr. King and Robert Kennedy. It was important to us that when we opened the place up in the morning and shut it at night we would do something that gave everything a little meaning. I guess it was almost like a little prayer. I can hardly remember my own home phone number on any given day, but I will never forget the code to the old City Year headquarters."

In a talk he gave once at his synagogue, Brown explained the deeply personal roots from which this philosophy emanates:

From my mother's Judaism, and her mother's, I received a love for ritual and community. Every Friday night my mother lit the Sabbath candles and wished us a good Shabbat. Every Passover the home was cleansed of chamatz. Every night of Hanukkah we lit the candles and thought of the bravery of the Macabees. And every day, our home was kosher, which always made our home special and spiritual. At Jewish summer camp, I learned to love the beauty of the havdala candles lit on the waterfront each Saturday night. . . .

Fundamentally, the way in which I have been developing our national service model at City Year is rooted in ritual that builds community, imparts meaning, and makes effective collective action possible. In fact, it was not until I had been working at City Year for several years, and developing scores of retreats, service projects, and techniques for reflection and learning, that I realized that the Passover Seder— with its universal theme of righteous exodus and its many rituals, beginning with the youngest child asking, "Why is this night different from all other nights?"—is perhaps the greatest example of "meaningful programming"—to use nonprofit jargon—that has ever been produced. It is so powerful that it has existed as a decentralized, home-centered annual event for more than two thousand years.

Brown argues that because City Year unites so many different young people, the need to create a new, inclusive culture is of primary importance. So all corps members wear uniforms and start each day with synchronized calisthenics, to physically demonstrate unity, spirit, and purpose. Each meeting at City Year begins with the sharing of "ripples"—stories from their work that give hope and inspiration.

At his synagogue, Brown quoted Tevye in *Fiddler on the Roof*: "Without our traditions, our lives would be as shaky as a fiddler on the roof!"

"For me," Brown continued, "the very idea of national service's enormous potential is rooted in the collective ritual of a nation's youth uniting for a shared, generational adventure in idealism—a civic rite of passage that builds the national identity and, after decades of civic deconstruction and confusion, can help reestablish a usable, inclusive, national civic culture."

City Year has not only developed rituals, it has studied its own history to extract learnings and captured those learnings with great discipline. Khazei summarizes the major ones this way:

- Remember that "every battle is won or lost before it is fought." This piece of wisdom comes from Sun Tzu's *The Art of War.* City Year translates it to mean "For better or worse, you always get the result you planned (or failed to plan) for." The three steps to winning battles before they are fought are to visualize a result, think backward, and implement forward.
- Decide what your core principles, values, and ideas are. Narrate them through everything that you do.
- Figure out what is fundamental to your vision, and do not compromise on that, no matter what the pressures are to do so. Be flexible, however, on everything else that is not essential to the vision— extremely flexible.
- Set what you believe to be achievable, realistic goals when starting out, and make sure that you meet or exceed every single one. It is essential to establish a strong track record of results and successes early on.

— Make all decisions with your ultimate vision in mind, but do not be worried if you cannot answer every question when you are just starting out. If the vision is strong and coherent, the path, to a degree, reveals itself.

— Leverage everything. All resources have multiple uses.

— Learn from your own experience. The learning curve in entrepreneurial organizations is steep, and your own experience can often be your best teacher.

— Remember the "Guardian Angel" axiom: If you are on the right path and are determined, you will have unexpected successes, unexpected good fortune, and "guardian angels" in the form of other people who will come out of the woodwork to help you.

The substance of each of these is less important than the fact that City Year has consciously studied and cataloged them.

III

City Year's achievement cannot be understood without acknowledging a third driving force, and like the third leg of a stool, he is the essential stabilizing force at City Year. Jeff Swartz was not a cofounder of City Year, nor was he a roommate of Alan or Michael. As chief operating officer of

Timberland, he was running a boot-and-clothing company that his grandfather had founded and his father owned, when someone at City Year called to ask for sixty pairs of boots. It was the beginning of an odyssey that resulted in Jeff investing millions of dollars and even more of his time, and ultimately agreeing to chair the City Year board.

At the age of thirty-six, Jeff Swartz has the business experience that every nonprofit organization craves. Before becoming chief operating officer of Timberland in 1991, he had also served as senior vice president of international sales and marketing, vice president of operations and manufacturing, and general manager of Timberland France and Timberland Europe. It was the kind of grooming that a CEO arranges for his heir apparent, which is exactly what Jeff was to Sidney Swartz, his father, himself the son of Nathan Swartz, the founder. Each has played a unique and complementary role. "My grandfather created a boot," Jeffrey often says. "My father created a brand. My contribution is to create a belief that is integral to both." When Jeff became CEO in 1998, Timberland had enjoyed seven consecutive quarters of improved earnings, was reporting revenues of $796.5 million, and had solidified its reputation as the reference brand for outdoor, rugged, high-quality footwear.

Business success has never been enough for Jeff. He told me once, privately, "I want so much, so badly, so urgently to live a life of value. . . . To repair the world, to put back together what we've brought apart, that is the work of heroic people."

Ken Freitas, vice president of social enterprise at Timberland and a close colleague of Jeff's, remembers how the
relationship with City Year started with a request for sixty
pairs of boots. After a series of meetings to explore working more closely together, they found: "We understand
things about the power of service, about diversity, about
leadership. Things that are very relevant to our business.
For the first time they take us through trainings, workshops,
about diversity, about workstyles. We understand things
that are very relevant for our business about creating value."

Freitas relayed another piece of the corporate history
about how Swartz, early in his tenure as COO,

> was wrestling with a certain problem and called on his rela-
> tionship with a board member named Dr. Abraham Zelez-
> nick. After dancing around the issue, trying to ask Zeleznick
> the question without officially asking him, Abe says, "Stop it.
> You're a typical young person. You think there's a right
> answer. There are no right answers, there are only beliefs. And
> what you have to do is you have to choose one. You have to
> choose well. And then you have to get behind it with every-
> thing you have. And then you have to get your organization
> to understand it, and get them behind it with everything
> that they have."

The result is a company like almost no other. In addition
to their substantial investment in City Year, Timberland
employees are given the opportunity to spend up to forty

hours of paid time per year participating in community-service activities. The company's commitment to community building contributed to Timberland's selection by *Fortune* magazine as one of the "100 Best Companies to Work For." During the annual four-day meeting of sales reps in Marco Island, Florida, the day that was usually devoted to golf and "spa work" was spent instead in Immokolee, Florida, the migrant worker capital of the South, building Habitat for Humanity homes and playgrounds and reading to first graders in their public schools. At dinner that evening, Jeff remained in the background, but one employee after another came to the microphone to give witness to how the experience had been a revelation, and why they felt so strongly about working for Timberland.

Jeff could not believe more strongly in the social responsibility of his company, but he also sees vital business needs being met: "Building community helps foster teamwork throughout the company, and helps to unify all Timberland employees toward a common, purposeful goal."

City Year is so convinced of the positive business outcomes that corporations will enjoy from this type of work that it has created an initiative called Care Force to arrange service projects and offer them for a fee to corporations and other institutions. To date, Care Force has organized programs, team-building initiatives, and training for more than 2,500 corporate employees and students, and has generated more than $100,000 in gross revenues. Care Force "clients" have included Bain & Company; Goldman,

Sachs & Co.; *Inc.* magazine; Babson College; and the American Society of Association Executives—just to name a few. Care Force holds the promise of becoming City Year's premier revenue-generating activity while simultaneously furthering the mission by engaging the private sector in service.

Jeff Swartz brings his own deep sense of cathedral building to the work. In a letter I received from him in July 1997, he explained:

> *One of my favorite sections in the Bible comes from Deuteronomy 30: 11–15, as Moses is charging the nation with how they "mayest" live their lives. Moses is facing his imminent death; as the leader he is, his concern is not for his individual fate, but for The Work that remains to be done after his death.*
>
> *To a nation accustomed to and in many ways dependent upon a leader who regularly and passionately intervened with G-d, who was the nation's link to Answers, Moses' wisdom is crucially important. He tells the nation that "this commandment that I command to you this day [the entire body of Torah law] is not remote from you. It is not in heaven so that you should say, 'Who shall go up to heaven and bring it to us.' Further, it is not over the sea so that you should say, 'Who will cross the sea and get it for us.' Rather it is something very close to you. It is in your . . . heart. See—today I have set before you a choice, between life and good, and death and evil." Moses' whole charge to the people is to recognize that only when individuals commit themselves to*

each other, only when each individual accepts his or her
responsibility as a human, only then is humanity capable of
transcendence.

IV

In 1991, presidential candidate Bill Clinton toured City
Year's Boston headquarters for the first time and talked
with corps members about their service. At the end of
that day, he declared, "I don't know if I'm going to be
president, but if I am president I know this is something
I'm going to do." From that day on, whenever candidate
Clinton pulled up to a rally in Boston or New Hampshire,
red-jacketed City Year corps members were there to greet
him with smiles and signs. When CYZYGY was held
in Providence, Rhode Island, last year, First Lady Hillary
Rodham Clinton was persuaded to come. When Eli Segal
went to meet the president to debrief him on the Welfare
to Work initiative, he brought with him five letters from
the five hundred that corps members had written. Segal
was Harris Wofford's predecessor running the Corporation
for National Service, and he remembers Clinton telling
him upon his appointment to the post in 1992, "I want you
to deliver for the rest of the United States what City Year
has done for Boston."

And so it was impressive, but not surprising, that at the
last hour the president of the United States overruled his

staff, and left behind the Oval Office, nuclear testing in India and Pakistan, the peace process in Northern Ireland, and the running battle with tobacco companies to board Air Force One to fly to Cleveland, where he would be met by Alan Khazei.

The president's schedule called for a stop at Steve Howell Elementary School before arriving at CYZYGY. Because of last-minute meetings with congressional leaders in Washington, he was already running late. City Year corps members kept the audience entertained with songs and stories. They competed to outcheer one another. They did their trademark calisthenics. The gym rocked with their energy. More than thirty national and local television news crews on risers at the back of the auditorium adjusted their cameras. Finally, to the strains of "Hail to the Chief," across the stage came Alan Khazei and President Bill Clinton.

The president was introduced by Leslie Frye, a nineteen-year-old corps member who serves people with AIDS at food pantries throughout Chicago. One of the five letters delivered by Eli Segal that had persuaded Clinton to come to Cleveland was handwritten by Leslie. She read it now as her way of introducing the president. She explained how her service had included work in an HIV/AIDS clinic, how she had seen people die and learned how people live. What she had written weeks before and read that afternoon embodied the idealism of every corps member in that room: "Mr. President, I hope that you are the person who is reading these next words. I hope that you see them with your own eyes and internalize them and realize what tremendous impact your decisions have on the lives of young people in America. Know, Mr. President, that because of your support there is a corps of sixty individuals in Chicago alone who will serve the community of humanity for life.

"Thank you, Mr. President, for believing in me," Leslie continued, as her voice began to break. It was as if she had unexpectedly become aware of something vital about herself. "Thank you for having the courage to stand up for who I am and the vision to see that I need you." She choked back a sob and paused, but only for a moment.

A young woman's breaking voice can be more contagious than a yawn. Don Baer, who until recently had been head speech writer for Clinton, was standing in the bleachers. He had heard the president introduced in every way imaginable; I would have thought him immune to sentiment. Tears pooled at the corners of his eyes and rolled down both cheeks. One bench above him stood Alan Khazei's wife, Vanessa. The distance between her and the president's podium held a decade of memories. She wept, too.

The president came to the podium, leaning into it, a hand gripping each side. "When I started running for president in 1991, I had this idea—but it was just an idea in my mind—that we had two big problems. We needed more idealistic, energetic young people out there working in our communities, helping to solve problems at the grassroots level and touching other children one-on-one . . . and we also needed to open the doors of college to everyone. So I had this general idea, and then, when I went to City Year in Boston, the lights came on in my mind, and I said, 'This is what I want to do!'"

Clinton's speech would be the highlight of the conference, but only because of who he was, not because of what he said. In fact, the rest of the speech fell wide of the mark. He began with a fairly standard recitation of what his aides must have insisted were the messages of the day: the tobacco companies must yield to reform, global warming must be paid attention to, the economy was strong. "I want the Congress and the country to accept changes in the earth's climate as real and commit ourselves to reduce the problem of global warming, even as we continue to grow the economy."

He ran through a litany of statistics like a musician who'd sung a song one too many times, forgetting that it was not just the words the audience wanted to hear, but what those words meant to him. Only toward the very end did he put down his prepared text and seem to remember to whom he was talking. "I am so proud of you. I can't even convey what it feels like for me to stand here and look into your eyes. I know now that one of the best decisions I ever made was to fight to create AmeriCorps and to fight to keep others from taking it away, and to fight to give you the chance to serve."

The president's delivery was flat. Whether worn down by the relentless investigation of the special prosecutor that plagued so much of his second term or just worn out by the demands of the Oval Office, he offered far from his best performance. It didn't matter to the corps members. The president had come to City Year to acknowledge what a decade of their sweat had accomplished. They cheered and cheered, and at the end they pressed against the rope line, a sea of red sleeves, to reach for his hand.

As infectious as Khazei's idealism is, some were clearly still immune. If the president missed the moment, so too did the local newspaper. Of the multitude of possible front-page headlines on this special day, *The Plain Dealer* chose PRESIDENT'S VISIT TO CAUSE MAJOR TRAFFIC HEADACHES.

Still, it was the day Alan Khazei had willed it to be, the day he had so long hoped for. But it was also a day, as the poet Seamus Heaney has written, when hope and history rhyme.

More than hope brought a president to City Year, more even than Alan's formidable will. In many ways, Clinton's visit was an acknowledgment that civic institutions like City Year, the Chicago Children's Choir, and Share Our Strength have reached a new level of maturity, a new readiness to effectively address social problems.

City Year's accomplishments have been formidable: engaging more than four thousand young people in full-time service, demonstrating the strength of diversity, and helping to build national service through AmeriCorps as a new national institution. But City Year's own strategic planners view themselves against the broader context of American history. There have been times, such as during the Progressive Era, when a plethora of vital new civic institutions were formed, like the American Red Cross, the Urban League, the Boy Scouts and Girl Scouts, and the YMCA. City Year is on the cusp of being such an institution. On the one hand, it operates in ten cities and matches every federal dollar with a private-sector dollar. On the other hand, its growth has slowed to just one city a year; it lacks the scale to attract national corporate partnerships and still lacks a well-defined brand image.

At the City Year board meeting in Cleveland, just prior to President Clinton's speech, Alan restated his intention to have the corps double to eighteen cities by the year 2000. His ambition is to demonstrate that a program with the characteristics and competencies of City Year can achieve scale, that it can secure the national service movement and develop a new cadre of social entrepreneurs.

The stakes are high, not just for City Year but for our democracy. Steve Waldman, author of a book called *The Bill,* documented the development and passage of the national service legislation that established AmeriCorps. He described national service as the "Swiss Army knife" of American democracy—a special institution that the nation keeps in its possession to achieve many important civic goals at once: service delivery, youth development, racial reconciliation, access to higher education, and citizenship development.

City Year has sought to leverage its own potential as a laboratory for "going to scale" into financial support from large funders. As it made the case to one anonymous donor:

The question of how to achieve scale remains a powerful and elusive one for promising nonprofit organizations, and more generally for the philanthropic community that supports them and for society at large. When all of the living presidents gathered at a summit in Philadelphia in 1997 to promote community service, President Clinton said that "the era of big government is over, but the era of big challenges is not, and therefore we must begin a new era of big citizenship." The success of the new era of big citizenship is, in a fundamental way, tied to the question of how small-scale, entrepreneurial, nonprofit organizations can be grown from innovative start-ups to high-impact, large-scale national operations.

In the private sector, a host of institutions and concepts bring the next Starbucks or Home Depot from a single shop to thousands of stores: seed capital, bridge capital, "going public," business schools, investment banks, consulting firms, not to mention the undeniable power of the profit motive to efficiently channel private investment into promising corporate ideas.

The nonprofit sector . . . has no such efficient set of institutions and concepts to maximize the potential of new ideas and organizations. . . . City Year can perhaps add critical knowledge and experience to the question of how to achieve scale for promising nonprofit organizations and ideas.

City Year, Share Our Strength, and many other organizations were founded in the mid-1980s. This is not just coincidence. This was dead center in the middle of the Reagan

years, when it became abundantly clear that the social
safety net would not be spared, even for those in greatest
need. Serious social problems would have to be addressed
by new community organizations because the institutions
that had once been set up to address them had either pulled
back or flat out given up.

And so for ten years, organizations like these have struggled just to prove their ideas worthy, and to survive. In this
first stage of their organizational life cycle, thoughts of
growing to scale were a luxury, as were conversations
about collaborating with others. That is very different now.
The work of community-based nonprofits has moved from
the periphery to the center of public affairs, and the challenge is no longer to prove that an idea works, but to prove
that those ideas that we know work can be taken to scale,
that they can make themselves felt across the entire nation.

John Gardner, the senior statesman and professor emeri-
tus at Stanford University, has written, "All citizens should
have the opportunity to be active, but all will not respond.
Those who do respond carry the burden of our free
society. I call them the Responsibles. They exist in every
segment of the community—ethnic groups, labor unions,
neighborhood associations, businesses—but they rarely
form an effective network of responsibility, because they
don't know one another across segments. They must find
each other, learn to communicate, and find common
ground. Then they can function as the keepers of the long-
term agenda."

What Gardner envisioned is finally coming to pass.

Many entrepreneurial organizations struggled so mightily to survive that even thinking about any type of collaboration would have been a luxury up until now. But with the stability and maturity that come with second-stage development, individual leaders and their organizations are increasingly coming together, jointly funding projects, sponsoring conferences, and sharing ideas.

"It doesn't happen overnight," John Gardner cautions. "A community is the child of time. I agree with William Drayton, who says that 'the conscious development of human institutions is the major evolutionary task.'. . .We have chronically underestimated the capacity of large-scale systems to resist change. We must design our efforts for the long haul. Short-term programs won't do it."

CHAPTER FIVE

A Pioneer of Community Wealth

I

Walla Walla, Washington, is a small city of less than thirty thousand at the foot of the Blue Mountains in the southeast corner of the state. Its entire population could be comfortably seated on one side of an NFL football stadium. It lies so close to the Oregon border that on a map, the second "Walla" almost spills across the state line. You can tell from the names of the surrounding geography that there was a time when life in this territory was not for the timid: Rattlesnake Flat, Ice Harbor Dam, Diamond Peak, Huntsville, Echo. Known today for little more than the Walla Walla Sweet Onion Harvest, it was once the largest city in what was called the Washington Territory.

Built by fur traders on the famous Native American Nez Percé trail, Walla Walla was officially founded in 1856, but it had seen Lewis and Clark's footsteps half a century earlier. The gold rush made it a commercial, banking, and manufacturing center, none of which outlasted the farms that still dominate its economy today. As one of the first areas settled between the Rockies and the Cascades, Walla Walla played a historic role in the development of the Pacific Northwest.

Walla Walla not only attracted the West's earliest pioneers, it bred a few as well. Gary Mulhair was born there in 1941. He spent his boyhood exploring the river valleys and working on farms. He can remember summers irrigating cornfields, pulling the pipes through thick rows of wet and heavy cornstalks and coming out drenched into the cold September air. In the fall, his mother sent him out to find and shell black walnuts that she wanted for cakes and pies. "They're very hard, and after cracking them, scraping the meat out of those was murder," he recalls. "Your fingers would be stained for maybe a week." She expected to receive the amount she'd asked for, often an entire bushel, no matter how hard it was or how long it took. From an early age, he understood that outcomes were what counted, that deliverables are how you measure value.

He stayed through college and eventually journeyed as far as Seattle, some 270 miles west, but no further. He never had to. The region's culture of rugged individualism has been defined by a spirited entrepreneurship and innovation that has changed the course of human history. Gary Mulhair helped do the defining. Many entrepreneurs have been at home there, from Bill Gates at Microsoft to Howard Schultz at Starbucks, as well as hundreds of others who are part of the region's flourishing high-tech economy. But when it came to social entrepreneurship, Gary Mulhair beat them all to the punch.

Since 1975, Mulhair has been creating jobs and saving lives through a unique model that is the envy of organizations across the nation. Under his leadership, Seattle's aptly named Pioneer Human Services has become the largest and most self-sustaining human service agency of its kind. He has revolutionized the way human service organizations operate through self-supporting enterprises and programs that integrate jobs, housing, training, and other support services for at-risk individuals. With revenues in excess of $50 million a year, Mulhair has created wealth of a magnitude previously unheard of in the nonprofit world.

He did it the toughest way possible, not by begging for foundation grants or government support, but by manufacturing and selling high-quality products and services with a workforce made up entirely of ex-offenders and former substance abusers. As he explained to the *Seattle Post-Intelligencer:* "These are people who have broken the law, folks most people are frightened of. They've been in prison or they're recovering from alcohol or drugs. They haven't held a job. When they apply for a job they get screened out pretty quickly. . . . We're going to hire people you wouldn't," Mulhair asserts, "but in a year or so, you will—because they'll be citizens."

What Pioneer's success means is that for the first time, a nonprofit organization is not dependent solely upon the charity of others. Its leaders do not have all of their

energies diverted and usurped by the relentless demands of fund-raising—the meetings, phone calls, dinners, and events designed to meet and win the hearts of
wealthy individual donors. Instead, they can focus on what
attracted them to the job in the first place: developing
effective programs to help the people they serve. Pioneer
has proved that nonprofits can do more than just redistribute wealth, which they are typically quite good at. They can
also create wealth, though it is a different kind of wealth—
community wealth—that is used to directly benefit the
community.

Shattering stereotypes is a fundamentally subversive
activity. Initially, Mulhair's role in inventing a new model
for nonprofits to grow to scale was so quiet as to be almost
unnoticed outside of the Seattle area. Running a factory,
building a profitable business, and delivering comprehensive social services to a severely challenged population—
all at the same time—is complicated, taxing work. Mulhair
couldn't find the time to both do the work and talk about
it, so he kept his focus on the former. Gradually, through
word of mouth, visitors, and the circulation of a few local
press clips, the story of what he'd accomplished began to
spread.

I called Gary Mulhair in 1996. I asked him to come to
Washington to join in a discussion about redefining civic
responsibility with people like Jeff Swartz of Timberland, former New Jersey senator Bill Bradley, and Michael
Kennedy from Citizen's Energy. Leaders in various fields
who were helping to create this new kind of community

wealth did not yet know one another, and were not shar-ing, collaborating, or even talking. Share Our Strength saw value in playing the simple role of convener.

"Why do you want me?" he asked with characteristic reticence. The tone of his voice was stern. I couldn't tell whether he was genuinely curious or whether the question was some kind of test, but I was conscious of choosing my words carefully.

"Because you've been doing what everyone else only talks about."

"Okay," he said, ending the conversation. It meant he would come.

I learned then that Gary doesn't usually say more than he needs to. But when he came to Washington a few months later, he said enough.

Fifty-six years old and neatly if conservatively dressed, he maintains a steady gaze through large round lenses as if searching for the real you and pretty much expecting to find it. He is cautious with his broad smile, but friendly in the way of a small-town pharmacist. You can trust that whatever he's telling you is for your own good. He's given to short declarative statements that you can take or leave.

In his plainspoken way, and without the pretense that usually accompanies a Washington presentation, Mulhair described for the group the history of Pioneer, which began in Seattle in 1962 when an attorney named Jack Dalton was released from prison after serving a sentence for embezzling from his clients. "Jack came out of prison," Mulhair explained, "and he realized he was disbarred, disowned, and disenfranchised. He had nothing going for himself except the fact that he had nothing going for himself. Along with half a dozen other former prisoners who were struggling to build new lives, he started a halfway house with a budget of less than a thousand dollars that he raised by going to the very friends from whom he had embezzled. Jack had a lot of chutzpah."

Pioneer now serves more than five thousand clients each year, employing nearly seven hundred people in its programs. Its largest business is a precision light-metal fabricator that has become the sole supplier to Boeing sheet-metal liners for the cargo bays of Boeing aircraft. On a visit there, I walked with Mulhair across a factory floor the size of a football field, listening to him chat with workers whose skills once included forging checks, trafficking cocaine, and burglary. He is able to explain each stage of the production process and how each custom-made machine operates. He describes the flow of water jets, laser cutters, and electrostatic paint machines as the workers move large, flat sheets of plastic and metal among them, cutting them into as many as three hundred precision pieces, depending on the configuration of the plane. "It's like a big jigsaw puzzle."

Thanks to Pioneer, this workforce of ex-offenders has acquired new skills in a first-rate production setting that offers the patience and support few conventional businesses can afford. Operating computer-controlled machine tools to fabricate parts according to designs transmitted electronically by their customers, the employees are held to the most exacting standards. I asked Mulhair what kind of problems they have on the factory floor with a work-force that has such a history as this one, assuming the prob-lems would be fighting and stealing. I assume wrong. "For about half of 'em, there comes a day where they just stop showing up. Problems with authority or what have you. That's about the only difficulty we have. But we can plan for it now and build it into the cost of doing business."

Mulhair is emphatic that quality is not sacrificed. He's got convincing evidence. In 1996, Pioneer's plant became the first nonprofit in the United States to win ISO-9002 certification, a benchmark for quality in the private sector. Even more convincing, Boeing keeps expanding its con-tract year after year.

In fact, Gary would argue that market forces ensure higher quality. As he told *The Chronicle of Philanthropy:*

Most of our activities are customer-driven, and it gives us a different relationship with the people we're providing ser-vices for than if we were getting government money or foun-dation money. What you care about when you are talking to a foundation officer is getting his or her money into your organization, and that's input-driven. Our activities are output-driven. . . . I don't think nonprofits in this country have done a very good job of understanding the management side of things, understanding that their businesses should succeed or fail not on how much money they raise, but on how good a job they do. And that means understanding who

*your customers are and always focusing on satisfying your
customers.*

Pioneer also operates a wholesale food distribution
enterprise that reaches four hundred food banks in twenty
states. Other businesses include a real estate division that
develops and manages more than 500,000 square feet of
residential and commercial properties, and the Mezza
Café—a 150-seat cafeteria for the corporate headquarters
of Starbucks. In 1986, Pioneer bought the St. Regis Hotel
in the heart of Seattle's popular Pike Place Market district.
Today, it has been transformed into an unusual hybrid, serving tourists on a budget and recovering substance abusers
participating in Pioneer's rehabilitation programs.

Ten years ago, 75 percent of Pioneer's revenues came
from government, mostly in the form of grants. Today, that
has been reduced to 25 percent, and most of that is from
government contracts for services. Fifty million dollars in
revenue is a lot of money for a nonprofit, and it attracts
more. The Ford Foundation just wrote a check for $2.4
million so that Pioneer can continue to acquire other businesses and convert them into sheltered nonprofit workshops. As a result, Pioneer bought Greater Seattle Printing & Mailing in Redmond, Washington, a six-million-dollar
business with lots of entry-level jobs, particularly on the
mailing and fulfillment side.

There is one fundamental reason that nonprofits have
only rarely started or owned businesses for the purpose of

generating revenues for growth and sustainability: They only rarely thought they could. It has been a colossal failure of imagination pervasive to the nonprofit sector. That's not to say there are not financial, managerial, and regulatory hurdles to overcome; there are in any business venture. But the limitations on nonprofits starting businesses have by and large been self-imposed.

Gary Mulhair managed to get around that. "Growing up in such a small town like Walla Walla made me feel that there were no limitations," he told me over dinner during a visit to New York. "I've never accepted that things had to be just one way or another."

II

Gary Mulhair finds himself in transition. The greatest demands on his time are no longer from customers or factory floor managers. They are from business-school professors, reporters, and human-services experts across the country who want to see what he has done and learn how it can be replicated. Foundations want him to consult with their grant recipients. Associations of nonprofits want him to keynote their conferences. He serves on boards and advisory committees ranging from the American Correctional Association to the Geese Theatre Company. It's not the role he expected to be playing.

Mulhair began his career at Pioneer as a staff consultant

running the business office and the Corrections Alcohol Drug Program. In 1979, he designed and built the Food Bank Buying Service, providing a cooperative whole-sale food and distribution service to almost one hundred northwest food banks. By then, Pioneer founder Jack Dalton had left the organization, though he served on Pioneer's board until his death. In 1983, Mulhair became director of finance and operations, managing agency needs and monitoring asset utilization.

"The long-term vision had been to create a self-supporting, outcome-driven, wealth-creating, entrepreneurial nonprofit organization. It took much longer than it should have to understand that the greatest constraint was getting highly capable people to share the vision. Having it myself was not enough. . . . I never really thought that resources would be difficult to obtain if the vision was understood."

Since then, Mulhair's vision has grown more expansive. Today, he hopes to transform the traditional model of corporate giving into a new philosophy that he calls "operational philanthropy." His plea to other businesspeople, through the pages of the *Puget Sound Business Journal:* "Instead of giving us money, give us work. We'll convert that to jobs and hire the people you won't hire. You'll receive products and services you need at a competitive rate."

Mulhair describes his business this way: "Our clients are recovering alcoholics and addicts coming out of prisons and jails, moms and crack babies, folks that never went to school, folks that don't have jobs. Our job is to create opportunity for them. We do that by recognizing all the limitations these folks bring to the table, and recognizing it takes a long time for them to change their lives." Pioneer structures its programs so that people can move through residences and enterprises over a two- or three-year period, all the while concentrating on making the business pay for itself.

The term "social entrepreneur" is in vogue today, but often goes conveniently undefined. To some, it means solving problems through the private sector rather than through government. To others, it implies a commitment to running your organization "like a business." And to some, simply being young and starting an organization qualifies as entrepreneurial.

Many define social entrepreneurs by the passion they bring to bear, but surely more than passion and youth are involved. I know lawyers, accountants, and car mechanics who are in their twenties and are passionate about what they do. But they are not entrepreneurs.

Being an entrepreneur, social or otherwise, requires something more. It must be defined as doing things in ways that have not been done before. This, in turn, often means taking risks, innovating, and experimenting, all of which are characteristic of entrepreneurs, but do not necessarily define them.

Mulhair doesn't talk much about being a social entrepreneur; he just goes about being one. "We try to find a customer to experiment on, and often it is Pioneer. We learn to provide price, quality, and service to ourselves, and then we go out and sell it to a third party. Give me the best management and the worst model, and I'll beat the best model and the worst management every time."

Gary is that most valuable of all teachers and preachers— a practitioner. He's that rare breed that waited to have a story to tell before going out and telling it. "I've always been a bit reluctant to play the role of leader. I was content to be an operator and to share the results."

Mulhair has gone beyond defining an agenda for the nonprofit sector. He's also been identifying the ingredients of how the business community can create community wealth. In discussing companies like Boeing and others who buy Pioneer's products, Mulhair wrote in the *Puget Sound Business Journal* that "when these companies contract to buy our products, they are creating a job opportunity for someone who desperately needs it. We call it 'operational philanthropy.' Many business people aren't used to thinking about using their vast purchasing power to meet philanthropic need. While they donate money generously, they fail to realize what an impact spending some of their vendor dollars on operational philanthropy could have. We need more companies to listen to our story and let us compete for the contracts they give to their vendors every day."

Through operational philanthropy, Boeing has almost certainly had a greater impact on issues surrounding ex-offenders and substance abusers than any foundation in the Pacific Northwest, and it has done so not through its philanthropy, but purely as a result of a purchasing decision.

What's easy to lose sight of in all of the excitement

about how Pioneer generates revenues is how those revenues are spent. Mulhair understands the complexities of helping people transition from drug and alcohol dependency. His philosophy is to wrap a cocoon around them through a blend of training, counseling, safe housing, a job, and careful monitoring to assure community safety. Pioneer is unique in offering all the services needed in one organization.

"My job is to create jobs," Mulhair explains. "I want people in my business, but when I get them in here, they come with a whole basket of problems, just a whole bundle of problems. We have to focus an enormous amount of attention on solving those problems—where are they going to live, keep them off drugs and alcohol, get them to work on time, get them to get along with their supervisor, get them reading skills."

As Mulhair concluded in a talk at a Stanford Business School conference on social enterprise: "My job is to add value to people by adding value to goods and services. . . . My job is not to please shareholders. I don't have any. What I have are people who need jobs and opportunity, and what they really want to add to themselves is economic value and social value. So our job is to facilitate that in as many ways as we can."

The implications of Mulhair's work are far-reaching. For nonprofits struggling to survive, the model is as seductive as water in the desert—maybe too seductive, for there is nothing easy or guaranteed on the risky path of starting a business. For those who aspire not only to survive but to thrive, it represents the essential missing link in their evolutionary progress. In the long term, if there is to be a long term for such organizations, there is simply no alternative. The choice they face is whether to fight for their share of the charitable pie, or to make that pie and their share grow.

If other organizations can be as successful as Pioneer, the wall between for-profit and nonprofit may soon become an anachronism. Gary Mulhair's work does not fit neatly into one category or another. Pioneer Industries is not a for-profit corporation. In fact, Mulhair admits, "Our strategies have involved ruthlessly exploiting our nonprofit status. We have learned to use all of the laws that are out there to reduce our operating costs. We are exempt from every imaginable business tax that I can find in the state of Washington: We run sheltered workshops that are exempt."

But with half a dozen businesses, seven hundred employees, and $50 million a year, Pioneer is not really a nonprofit either, except in the most technical, legal sense of the word. Instead, it is something new, something we don't have tax laws and regulatory bodies for, at least not yet. It is a community-wealth enterprise.

What Mulhair built took twenty years. He is not finished, but he is already the reference point for all of those who follow, a pioneer of community-wealth enterprise. He succeeded where others have failed, and his success is at an order of magnitude greater than anyone else who ever succeeded in the same field. Changing the rules of our free-market economy cannot be done from one annual report to the next. It is not the work of a single career. It is necessarily the work of a lifetime, or of several lifetimes, which Mulhair seems to have implicitly understood.

I asked Mulhair what served as his specific inspiration: "This has been almost entirely internally driven. It seems to come from imagining 'states' that I think are desirable (i.e., things I think should be that aren't) and then being motivated to achieve the things that are imagined. This process, for me, involves mentally identifying obstacles to what it is I want to achieve. The internal motivation comes from trying to imagine all the ways to overcome the obstacles without compromising anything. Essentially, I'm competing against myself, and I'm motivated by the internal competition."

Nancy Carstedt's experience with the Chicago Children's Choir was described as special, but not uncommon. Thousands of organizations are similarly situated. The same cannot be said for Pioneer. It stands out as one of a kind, much the way the cathedral of Milan does among Italy's multitude of churches. This is cathedral building at work. All of the ingredients are there:

 — a vision of what can be rather than what is
 — working back from that envisioned outcome, rather than measuring input
 — integrating diverse materials and resources into an architecture that fits, and understanding that they are all needed, not just one
 — devotion to a task that spans an entire career because

the job couldn't really be accomplished right in less than that time

- recognition that everyone has value to add, that everyone has a strength to share

These, indeed, are the ingredients of something magnificent, something that counts, something that lasts.

III

Pioneer Human Services was not the first example of community-wealth creation in the country. It is just one of the largest, and arguably the most impressive. Mulhair's work at Pioneer paralleled a virtual explosion in this type of innovation and entrepreneurship among those leading social change efforts in the United States.

As nonprofit organizations in every American community are scrambling to bridge gaps in federal social spending, they're turning to the business sector, not for donations but to create their own sources of revenue. The most innovative ideas are emerging from unlikely places. An order of Roman Catholic priests produced a feature film, *The Spitfire Grill,* that captured the Sundance Film Festival Audience Award. The $4 million profit from its sale to Castle Rock Entertainment will help to support the social service programs of the church.

Such efforts come in several different varieties. Business

enterprise is just one type. For example, Minnesota Public Radio sold its catalog business to the Dayton Hudson Corporation for an estimated $120 million. About three fourths of the proceeds—$90 million—will be added to the nonprofit's endowment.

Other organizations have pursued licensing or cause-related marketing partnerships that have proved lucrative and furthered their ability to expand operating capacity.

The range of activities is breathtaking:

— The National Trust for Historic Preservation raises revenues through study tours in the United States and abroad, and through the sale of reproductions of historic furniture.
— New Community Corporation in Newark, New Jersey, was founded by Monsignor William Linder to provide social services and create jobs. To fund its activities—and employ city residents—it opened much-needed retail, banking, real estate, and food services. The Corporation also manages a for-profit fine-dining restaurant in a converted Gothic church. These ventures provide the resources to run a nursing home that employs 240 people, a group of seven day-care centers that employ another 240, and a home health-care program that employs 160. "We also started our own business-loan fund and a low-income-housing tax-credit pool for smaller nonprofit organizations in the state, so that they can become more competi-

tive," reports Linder. "Last year was our first year, and we did $12 million. We expect to do $25 million this year."

– Store of Knowledge, based in Los Angeles, is a for-profit chain of retail stores located in shopping malls across the country. Almost every new store is opened in partnership with a local public broadcasting station. In fact, the original concept for the chain came from a Los Angeles public broadcasting station, KCET. The local public television affiliate contributes its reputation, name, logo, and promotional support in exchange for a percentage of sales and an equity stake in the store. Store of Knowledge, Inc., contributes the start-up and operating capital along with all of the functions necessary to run the retail operation. The company will operate more than sixty-five retail stores and expects sales to reach $100 million by the end of 1998. If the company goes public, its public broadcasting partners expect a solid financial return—the company has been profitable from the start. Store of Knowledge's partnerships create a competitive advantage. As Paul Gainer, vice president of general merchandise, says, "People identify us as the local station's store. That's what separates us from other toy stores."* Gary Ferrell, executive vice president for business development and chief financial officer for

*The Wall Street Journal, "Public TV Toy Stores Target the Cerebral," December 8, 1997.

KCET, says, "Our community perceives the Store of Knowledge as another way that the station reaches out and touches the community. Although it's a purely for-profit company, they view it as another way that KCET serves its community."

— Asian Neighborhood Design was founded in 1973 by community-minded architecture students at the University of California at Berkeley who wanted to improve living conditions in San Francisco's Chinatown. The organization provides low-income communities with housing, tenant education, and job training. Its construction and cabinetmaking business, Specialty Mills Products, generates $2 million of its $5.2 million budget. They have manufactured woodwork and other fixtures for residences, commercial businesses, and offices throughout California.

— Housing Works, Inc., provides housing, health care, job training, job placement, and a wide array of support services to men, women, and children living with AIDS or HIV in New York. Through thrift shops and a used-book café they had projected sales in 1997 of $5 million, and they employed forty-five people.

— The Nature Conservancy, which is the nation's twentieth-largest charitable institution and its largest conservation organization, launched a joint venture with the Vermont Land Institute to purchase twenty-seven thousand acres of timberland in

New York and Vermont that will be managed as a commercial demonstration project to show that land can be commercially logged without damaging watershed and wildlife. John Sawhill, the president of the Nature Conservancy, told *The Wall Street Journal,* "We have got to demonstrate that you can earn an economic rate of return on land while also protecting biodiversity." In a hint of what might be to come, he added, "It's not only in forestry, but also in agriculture, oil drilling, and ranching."

The potential now exists to transform the role that the civic sector plays in society, and to transform the way the nonprofit and corporate communities work together by literally creating community wealth through business enterprise, cause-related marketing partnerships, and licensing—directing profits back into the community. The challenge now is to advance this concept.

IV

I asked Gary Mulhair how he fueled his own creative process. His tenure at Pioneer had been marked by one innovation after another, the only visible pattern being adapting ideas from one sector and making them work in another. He explained: "The really important learning source for me has been a wide-ranging reading list that includes history, biography, science fiction, natural sciences, business, periodicals, and newspapers. I'm not quite sure how it works in my mind, but the creative or learning process seems to be driven by taking in as much and as varied information as I can. It seems to percolate until insight occurs. I liken the insight to connecting the dots and seeing patterns and opportunities where others just see chaos."

His answer fits squarely with an insightful and long-established theory of creativity I learned through Joel Fleishman, one of the most compassionate and important thinkers and leaders in the effort to help nonprofit organizations grow to scale.

It is sometimes unfairly seductive to think of our newer friends as wiser than our older ones, but in the case of Joel Fleishman this is true. He has been on the law faculty of Duke University for nearly three decades, and he also directs their Center for Ethics at the Terry Sanford Institute of Public Policy. The boards he serves on are as diverse as the Schechter Institute of Jewish Studies in Jerusalem, the John and Mary Markle Foundation, and Harvard's Joan Shorenstein Barone Center on Press, Politics and Public Policy. He has authored numerous articles on philanthropy, urban studies, and public financing of elections, and he was wine columnist for *Vanity Fair* for eight years.

After a relatively brief introduction to Share Our Strength, Joel suggested, in a manner gentle as ever, a book by Arthur Koestler: "He has this theory of creativity which is really what your work is evidence of."

Koestler's theory goes by the clumsy name "bisociation theory," and is described in his book *The Act of Creation*. Its essence is that all acts of creation involve the mental conjunction of two previously separate ideas. Bisociation is the act of combining two ideas from different worlds to create something new. Gutenberg's invention of movable type is a good example. Having already been familiar with the idea of carving letters into small individual blocks, it took participating in a wine harvest and noticing the pressure exerted by the wine press to combine the idea of movable type and the printing press. The prescription for creativity, almost exactly as Mulhair described, is to have a wide range of interests to increase the likelihood of two disparate ideas coming together. The importance of Koestler's work is that it refutes the notion that creativity is confined to accidents of birth or genius, and argues instead that it can be nurtured, and that we know what the specific conditions are for nurturing it well.

This is something that chefs almost uniquely (not accidentally, I now realize) do every day. They combine ideas that simply haven't been combined before. Consider *New York Times* food writer Marian Burros's description of one of the most admired chefs in the United States, Michel Richard:

Michel Richard strode into his kitchen one morning last week and announced,"I want to make French toast." . . .

He stuffed them [two ordinary slices of white bread] with a slice of crème brûlée, welded them together with a paste of confectioners sugar and water, then dipped the "sandwich" in beaten egg and sautéed it in butter. For a finishing touch he dusted it with confectioners sugar and then browned it with a blow torch.

The next morning he was at it again, this time with caramelized apples between two very thin slices of bread and no egg dip. Finally it was coming together. Mr. Richard was onto something.

Moving from one experiment to another, he soon had his chef de cuisine, Stephan Beauvallet, poaching fish in olive oil. Then he was spooning lemon olive oil over vanilla ice cream. Impossible to explain why, but it tasted superb. That's Michel Richard.

Bisociation is not uncommon to chefs. Another example, this time one that had a positive impact on the public interest, came about this way:

Even traveling in first class, Monique Barbeau was wary of other airline passengers. She'd been bothered too often by flirtatious businessmen. She preferred to sit alone, read, and mind her own business. So when Dean Kasperzak, handsome, boyish, and well-tailored, sat down next to her, she avoided eye contact. But there was no way Dean could have known this, and accordingly he was undeterred. The irony was, this time there really was something to talk about. They were each in a business that, in a way, depended upon the other.

Barbeau is one of the best chefs in the country, and when she is not at her acclaimed restaurant, Fullers, at the Seattle Sheraton Hotel & Towers, she is acting as guest chef or cooking at benefits for charity. With just a trace of an accent from her native Canada and more than a trace of a smile, she is quick to engage, and hold her own with, anyone.

Kasperzak was the vice president of Calphalon, a leading producer of high-quality cookware and kitchen accessories based in Perrysburg, Ohio, and founded in 1963 by his father, Ronald M. Kasperzak. Originally, the company produced a quality line of heavy-duty aluminum cookware for the food-service industry. In the late 1960s, Calphalon developed a hard-anodized heavy-duty aluminum cookware line that made the cooking surface stick-resistant. The company distributed this new cookware, called Calphalon, through the food-service market to gourmet chefs. Because Calphalon markets itself as "the professional cookware," getting chefs like Monique Barbeau to use its products is no small part of Dean's job.

Once the conversation wandered into comfortable territory, it wasn't long before Barbeau told Dean about Share Our Strength. She had participated in Taste of the Nation benefits, and she immediately saw opportunities for partnership that would benefit both SOS and Calphalon. She encouraged Dean to get together with me, and we did.

At that first meeting, Dean gave me an energetic, enthusiastic briefing on Calphalon, speaking continuously for about thirty minutes about products, employees, market share, and profitability. Then he stopped and exhaled a deep sigh. "But look, it's just pots and pans," he said.

For Dean, something was missing. For SOS, an opportunity was born.

I told him about the work of Share Our Strength, how we find ways for individuals and companies to contribute through their skills, to literally share their strength. We both recognized that it would be great to work together, but we didn't have specific ideas about what form that might take. After a few hours of discussion, we went our separate ways.

In about ten days, Dean called me from his office near Toledo. In a completely different tone of voice from "but it's just pots and pans," he said, proudly, "Our strength to share is that we make pots and pans. And we want to make one for SOS." I wasn't sure what he had in mind, but I liked the way he was thinking.

Dean proposed that Calphalon refashion its two-quart sauté pan and market it as the Taste of the Nation pan. They would license the Taste of the Nation trademark that we owned and pay us a royalty of five dollars per unit sold. Sure, I thought. The Taste of the Nation pan? Go knock yourself out. It sounded like the most ridiculous thing I'd ever heard. Why would anyone want to buy something called "the Taste of the Nation pan"?

Calphalon ended up selling about four times as many of those pans as they'd sold the year before. In that first year alone, Share Our Strength received royalties of $180,000. The partnership worked because we spent a lot of time at Calphalon trying to understand what made pots and pans sell for them. What we learned is that a key ingredient is their relationship with their major retailers. So we constructed a three-party relationship. Calphalon licensed our

trademark, the major department stores like Blooming-
dale's and Macy's positioned the product front and center
of their cookware sections, and Share Our Strength was
contractually obligated to bring the best chefs in every
city—Monique Barbeau and her colleagues—into those
department stores to do cooking demonstrations.

When it came time for us to receive that first royalty
check of $180,000, Dean Kasperzak asked if I would come
to their headquarters in Toledo, Ohio, to accept the check
at a ceremony in front of their employees. A ceremony was
organized in the company auditorium. As Dean took the
podium, he talked about how proud Calphalon was of the
role they'd played in our hunger efforts, and as he handed
me the check and we shook hands, he said into the microphone: "I hope this money has a big impact on your hunger
relief efforts and that it will really make a difference in
your work." I took the microphone to assure him it would
and to add a word of thanks. As we were walking off stage,
he leaned a bit closer and said, much more quietly, in a
stage whisper really, "If we're giving you $180,000, can
you imagine how much *we* made?"

That was exactly the relationship Share Our Strength
wanted to have with Calphalon. The benefits to them were
so clear and compelling, so directly tied to their own profitability, that they had as strong a vested interest in its con-
tinuation and success as we did. It was a partnership that
created new wealth. As a result, it was sustainable over
time. The best evidence of this is that years later, the relationship has continued even after Calphalon was acquired

by Newell, a larger housewares company, and even after Dean Kasperzak left Calphalon.

As valuable as the ongoing royalties have been for SOS, that is probably not the most important part of the experience. As I left the Calphalon auditorium that afternoon and unexpectedly cut through the office building on the way to the parking lot, I saw something that felt every bit as good as the $180,000 check in my breast pocket. The screen saver on many of the employees' computers was the SOS logo, and there were antihunger posters in the employee lounge and on the poster boards hung in their cubicles.

The lessons learned at Calphalon were profound. They were a small blue-collar company in Toledo, Ohio, that made great pots and pans. That was their mission. They never contemplated playing a major role in ending hunger across America, nor did they have any desire to be considered as socially responsive along the lines of a Ben & Jerry's or The Body Shop, but they learned something surprising. The type of community involvement they always thought might be nice but too costly to afford had actually turned out to be quite profitable. In every year since that first one, the initiative to expand the relationship has come from Calphalon, driven not by Share Our Strength's need for additional dollars to fight hunger but by Calphalon's chief financial strategists telling senior management that this is good for their business.

As Dean Kasperzak testified one night in New York following a black-tie awards dinner and three strong martinis: "I used to be a pot-and-pan salesman, but now, because of what we've done together, I'm a tuxedo-wearing, community-wealth-building, pot-and-pan salesman."

If Calphalon can be engaged in such a community-wealth-building partnership, so too can any company in the country. What it takes is the creativity that comes with taking ideas from one sector and making them work in another, and a commitment to structuring a partnership in ways that are truly mutually beneficial.

History is replete with powerful examples of ordinary people using skills honed for one craft or trade for an entirely different purpose, at times extraordinary in its impact.

Consider a collection of rare photographs called "The Illegal Camera." I read about it in a *New York Times* review of a traveling exhibition of such photos. They were more than half a century old and depicted what came to be known as "The Hunger Winter." That caught my interest, but only hinted at the incredible drama behind these pictures.

On May 10, 1940, German troops entered and began a long occupation of the previously neutral Netherlands. Over the next five years, the Netherlands lost more of its Jewish population than any other Western European country. At the war's end, only twenty-seven thousand Jews had survived from a pre-occupation population of 140,000. As the German military presence and subsequent roundup of Jews to concentration camps increased, German civil law was imposed, restricting photographers from shooting or publishing any unapproved subject.

An underground resistance developed. By working from secret vantage points or hiding their cameras in coats and bags, Dutch photographers were able to document, albeit in oddly tilted and blurred photos, the tragic developments in their country. One of the most tragic came during the winter of 1945, one of the coldest on record. The shortage of food resulting from the German occupation, strikes, and evacuations brought severe starvation and death, especially in large cities like Amsterdam. The underground photographers not only sought to record their images for posterity, but courted even greater danger by smuggling them to England to convince the exiled Dutch government and the Allied forces to authorize food drops to alleviate the suffering.

The black-and-white images themselves—a boy with bony legs sticking out from his nightshirt, six emaciated bodies awaiting burial, a woman struggling to raise a crust of bread to her mouth—are horrible and sad, but they are not nearly as remarkable as what we don't see, just inches from the lens: the photographers themselves, who accepted the gravest possible risks to their lives and their families to tell the world of hunger. They had no money, no weapons, no legal right to conduct their work, but they had the power to bear witness, as do we all, and they had the courage to use it.

America faces a "hunger winter" of a very different sort. The repeal of welfare and cuts in food stamps, including $14 billion from the three million families who fall below the poverty line (making less than $6,200 a year), will take food away from children and send some of them into the streets. Millions will be hungry in the months ahead.

Hunger here is due to poverty, ignorance, and injustice. There is, of course, no comparing this to the unparalleled horror of the Holocaust. But there is inspiration to be taken from the handful of brave patriots who knew that for all they couldn't do there was one thing they could, and that was to see and tell a story that needed to be told. In our country, the camera is not illegal. We have not only the power but the right to see, to tell, to speak out, to insist that our fellow citizens take notice and act. We have hunger close to home. What we don't have is an excuse for silence.

Today's leaders don't want to risk a campaign contribution or a single percentage point in the polls, let alone their careers or lives, to speak out on behalf of the politically incorrect hungry. In truth, there weren't many that stuck their necks out fifty years ago about the suffering in Europe. There certainly weren't enough. But there were a few, a handful who knew that for all they couldn't do there was one thing they could, and that was to see and tell a story that needed to be told then, and maybe even more so now.

Near the end of the exhibition, there is one picture that was taken out in the open, of a small parade on the day after the Netherlands was liberated. Three young boys in short pants and tailored coats are standing on an empty cobblestone street alongside a canal. Their coats are torn and tattered. The smallest one is standing in front waving a flag, and the two behind him are banging sticks across the top of large tin boxes. Their smiles are tentative, fragile, as if not sure this moment of freedom can last. If you look very closely at the tin boxes they have fashioned into drums, you can see the stenciled letters on the sides of the air-dropped provisions: WELFARE BISCUITS.

If there is a time to come in this country when children who were once scared and hungry can joyously beat drumsticks against the welfare packages they no longer need, it will be because Americans have recognized that there is a role for everyone in the battle to save our children and build better communities. Whether we are rich or poor, black or white, educated or unskilled, each of us has at least the strength to do one personal but profound thing: bear witness to a common vision of what decency and humanity can mean.

The Dutch photographers' pictures show what hunger looked like half a century ago, under extraordinary, unprecedented circumstances. But if you look carefully—indeed, if you look beyond them—you can see straight through to what a courageous heart could achieve then, now, and ever.

Ordinary people using skills they'd taken for granted, but putting them to a new purpose in an extraordinary way—bisociation is one name for it, cathedral building another. Either way, the results are the same.

CHAPTER SIX

"We Are Now Challenged to Be Institution Builders"

I

Of the $60 million that Share Our Strength has raised and distributed to fight hunger and poverty over the last decade, more than $32 million has come from the annual Taste of the Nation food and wine benefit. It is the organization's flagship, with nearly a hundred of these events taking place at about the same time each year in cities across the country. Nearly five thousand chefs participate by preparing taste-size portions of their signature dishes, which are enjoyed by more than sixty thousand participants. With the chefs donating their time and all of the food, and 100 percent of the ticket proceeds going directly to antihunger agencies, it embodies all of the values of sharing strength.

Some of the events, like Atlanta's, are black-tie affairs at the city's finest hotel. Others are outdoors along the river, as in Richmond, or at the train stations in Washington and

Cincinnati. The National Cowboy Hall of Fame is the forum for Oklahoma. In New York, the chefs have served on the yacht *New Yorker* as it cruises around the Statue of Liberty. Typically, each year I try to visit those I haven't been to, in order to learn what's new and different. In contrast to the early years, when I carried food trays and took tickets at the door, my role now is a relatively easy one: no heavy lifting, just thanking the volunteers and sponsors and making a few remarks so that attendees get a fuller sense of the impact they are having on their community.

Scheduling constraints permit me to attend only nine or ten of the hundred events held around the country each year, but year after year, I go back to the event in Denver. I don't go just because Denver held Share Our Strength's first Taste of the Nation event back in 1987 or because it's one of the biggest and best events. In fact, I don't go for professional reasons at all.

I fly to Denver every year because there is a small, shy man with a salt-and-pepper beard and the slightest trace of an Irish accent whom I will get to be with for a few hours. Being with him, no matter how briefly, will make me better than I was before. Like life's blood cycled through the heart until it is oxygenated rich and red again, whatever ideals or hopes were tired and depleted inside me will come back robust and full from my time with him. When the needle of my own moral compass begins to waver, the pull of his moral force keeps me at true north.

His name is Noel Cunningham, and his appearance is deceiving. In his restaurants (over the years he's owned as many as three at one time), at events, and at meetings during the day, Noel walks into a room wearing chef's whites and stained checked pants with the same modesty that Gandhi exhibited wearing a white cloth wrap. His face is capable of many expressions: seriousness of purpose, impatience, a merry smile that says "I know exactly how to make you happy and you're about to find out yourself." His eyes carry the pain of suffering he sees right in front of him, or of that which he has been made aware even half a world away. Unlike the rest of us, his vision does not blur the farther out he looks. Those eyes, when concerned about another's welfare, are like alarm bells that cannot be ignored. His shoulders are slightly stooped as if carrying even more than the weight of his own burdens: a father lost to alcoholism, a brother lost to AIDS, custody of a sister-in-law's young children.

But don't mistake the strength of that spine. When a fellow board member once used his work with SOS to get some publicity for himself and enhance his stature among his business colleagues, it was Noel who looked him straight in the eye from across the boardroom table and said quietly, sadly, "Maybe it is time for you to go." Try to reduce funding for the projects of villagers in Haiti or Cambodia, and Noel will wait until everyone has spoken before making the case: "What it appears to me is that we're taking the easy way out and cutting funds from the people who don't have a voice at this table, and that would be just a goddamned disgrace if you don't mind me saying so, and the beginning of SOS losing its soul."

In 1987, I moved to Colorado to work in Senator Gary Hart's presidential campaign. SOS was less than three years old. The whole organization was still small enough—just my sister Debbie and one other staff person—to be carried around with me like a turtle carries his home on his back. When we were headquartered in Washington, D.C., being new and one of ten thousand nonprofits, our obscurity was assured. Our work did not really impact the city where we lived, and for all intents and purposes, we were ignored. Denver, on the other hand, embraced us warmly. Everyone we turned to for help recommended that we contact the local restaurant critic, Pat Miller, and the chef of the popular restaurant Strings, Noel Cunningham. Between them, they had an extensive network of contacts, and they were the keys, we were told, to getting anything done.

Pat, also known as The Gabby Gourmet, had a popular three-hour radio show every Sunday morning during which people called to talk about their dining experiences of the previous Saturday night. The comments could make or break a restaurant. She was both influential and good to her friends in the dining industry. Her best friend of all was Noel.

My sister and I called Pat, and within the hour we were sitting in her living room in southeast Denver, listening to her tell Noel that he needed to help us. Although they were two of the busiest people in Denver, you would have thought we were the first to have ever asked anything of them. There was not a moment's hesitation. Their time was now ours, as were their homes and businesses. They believed the best way to leverage their value to us was to reach out to their colleagues so that the city's entire restaurant industry was united behind our goals. They committed 100 percent on the spot and delivered 200 percent. In record time, the date and location had been set for a Taste event, the first in a program that, just one year later, would grow to include twenty-five cities. We spent so much time together, we eventually had to stop eating at Strings, because Noel would never let us pay.

There have been eleven years of such days so far. Noel Cunningham committed his life to ending hunger. It was a quiet commitment manifested in action, not words, the deeply internal kind of commitment a champion athlete must make during all the years of practice before breaking an Olympic record. Noel just devoted a greater and greater portion of each and every day to talking with customers, wait staff, suppliers, and fellow restaurateurs about how their contribution of $1,000, $100, or even a quarter could make a difference. He cooked at benefit dinners around the country. He wrote letters to Congress, the president, the television networks. The lack of response did not deter him in the slightest. He contacted other chefs in other cities to ask why they were not involved. He committed his life, its length, to ending hunger because he knew that anything less could not succeed.

Noel's commitment changed Share Our Strength, but more important, it changed Denver and the soup kitchens and homeless shelters there. It changed children's hospitals and school breakfast programs across the United States. It helped establish food and seed-and-irrigation systems in Eritrea, El Salvador, and a dozen other countries. Whenever I think of the impact of the Chinese student standing alone in front of a tank in Tiananmen Square, I also think of the impact of an Irishman standing alone in front of a grill, spatula in hand. He just hasn't had his picture taken yet.

Noel understood that the most popular restaurant in town is not a bad base for persuading people to give something back to their community. The bank president might be at lunch there one day with the owner of an oil company. A senator and the editor of the morning paper might have dinner there the next. A chef who knows how to leverage complimentary appetizers and desserts, and who is always welcome to drop by a guest's table, can get a lot done in a day. He'd tell them about our events, our need for sponsorship money, cars, volunteers, donated food, and wine. "Hey, whatever you can do," he'd say with a shrug, making it hard not to do something.

It was a far cry from where Noel started: an airport restaurant in Dublin, Ireland. Learning how to cook at age fourteen from his uncle, who was a chef, Noel craved formal training. He got it at London's Savoy Hotel, where executive chef Louis Virot mentored him. A degree in culinary arts from Westminster College was squeezed in on days off, his first formal education since leaving school in fifth grade.

Noel says it was a trip to Disneyland for his twin girls that brought him to the United States in 1976. That's probably only half true. The twins were probably just an excuse. Disneyland is for dreamers. It is not the world as it is, but the world as it could be. Disneyland was invented for Noel Cunningham. That vacation turned into a ten-year mastery of California cuisine, and then the dream of his own restaurant in Colorado.

Everyone has their own story about Noel's commitment to Share Our Strength. For my sister Debbie, the associate director of SOS, it is the time he came to Washington for the launch of the Charge Against Hunger campaign. "American Express had agreed to donate three cents to SOS every time you used your American Express card to pay for food and drinks in a restaurant. The night we went to dinner to celebrate, he paid for each individual beer and appetizer with his American Express card so that we could generate more transactions."

Noel has a way of boiling big, insurmountable problems with seemingly complex solutions down to very simple questions with very simple answers. For example, during the Rwandan crisis, he asked his customers to pay for their water. This represents so many facets of his "naively savvy" approach. It was symbolic, in that water is something most of us take for granted. It was easy, no bones about it—it was very simple. It was his response to the "call" he felt upon hearing the news of the suffering going on. It re- flected his abiding faith in humanity; that his customers would do the unthinkable and *pay* for tap water was never a question in his mind. He created the perception that it would be unthinkable *not* to.

During an SOS trip to Eritrea, at every stop Noel always closed things out by asking the host, "In a perfect world, what's your dream for this program/health center/ orphanage/dam/village?" And usually, their biggest dreams were things that were readily available in the United States. One former military official told him they needed more vehicles to move people and supplies, and Noel came right back and talked to the Denver Jeep dealer.

Noel Cunningham is a great chef and successful businessman, but that's not what has made him such a powerful force in the battle against hunger. He is personally the most generous human being I've ever met, buying plane tickets, meals, cars, and even homes for people he knows who are in need. But his generosity accounts for only a small piece of the impact he has had.

His power comes from two things: his vision, and his commitment to remain true to that vision no matter how naive it may seem or how uncomfortable it may make others at times. If some people see the glass of water as half empty, or half full, then Noel sees the need for "a bigger goddamned glass"—one that his customers should pay for.

Koestler's bisociation theory of creativity comes naturally to the great chefs. Putting disparate ingredients together to create something new is what they do. They will try anything once, which is exactly the attitude Noel Cunningham brings to his work with SOS. He has a rationale for even the most wildly ambitious ideas—Coke and Pepsi working together for SOS; NBC, ABC, and CBS interrupting their regularly scheduled broadcasts to report on Taste of the Nation; Michael Jackson or Barbra Streisand donating the proceeds of their next concerts to SOS. There is no arguing with his appeal to at least try. "What's it going to cost you? Thirty-three cents?" he asks, referring to the cost of sending a letter to Dan Rather. "What's the worst that can happen? They'll say no?"

Noel's goodness is not always practical, but it is always authentic, and this authenticity moves people further than anyone would have guessed they were capable of being moved. Noel's authenticity serves him the way martial arts might serve a fighter, as leverage to compensate for the lack of other strengths. It is so real, so undeniable, that it compels others to believe that there must be at least some of that same goodness in themselves, and thereby compels them to the same actions as Noel's. His impact on people is similar to Billy Budd's as described by Herman Melville: "A virtue went out of him, sugaring the sour ones."

To appropriate another American author, I suspect Noel's response to something as pretentious as a philosophy would be much like what John Steinbeck wrote in a letter to his biographer: "As to the question as to what I mean by—or what my philosophy is—I haven't the least idea. And if I told you one, it wouldn't be true. I don't like people to be hurt or hungry or unnecessarily sad. It's just about as simple as that."

II

On Sunday, August 2, 1998, I flew yet again to Colorado for the annual Taste of the Nation event which was being held at Coors Field for the second year. More than forty-five hundred people showed up, filling an entire deck circling the stadium. It was Denver's largest Taste event ever. Unfortunately, I wasn't one of the forty-five hundred. My United Airlines flight from Washington's Dulles Airport pulled away from the gate and then sat on the runway for three hours.

When we finally landed in Colorado, a forty-dollar taxi ride got me to the stadium exactly one minute after the event ended at 8:00 P.M. Walking in with my suitcase and computer as everyone else was walking out guaranteed a few sympathetic looks that were met by a sheepish smile. The green ball field sparkled behind the now empty restaurant stations, and you could see what a spectacular backdrop it provided under blue skies. But other than someone spilling an entire bottle of Coors on my laptop, I didn't really have the sense of participating.

Arriving late also gave me my first chance to view those who attended from a slightly different angle and perspective than usual. There were a lot of happy faces coming out of the ballpark, and not just because the food was good. Taste of the Nation always exceeds expectations. I've seen more sesame-encrusted salmon and crème brûlée in a month than most people see in a lifetime. We go beyond customer satisfaction, to what management gurus call "customer delight." Our "customers" get more "value" than they expect. When they see others participating in large numbers, they also get the fulfillment of having genuine impact fighting hunger. The fact that not a penny is kept by SOS, but is instead distributed to nearby antihunger agencies, makes this event even more appealing to those who participate.

The participating chefs and wineries who are literally sharing the strength know that they've given in a way that no one else could. Almost anyone can write a twenty-five-dollar check to Share Our Strength. Almost anyone can serve trays or ladle soup at a soup kitchen. But not many of us could cook gourmet food at a fancy event. These chefs can, and they sense how special the contribution is. That's why for eleven consecutive years now, Taste of the Nation has continued to raise more money than it did the year before.

The committee of volunteers that organized the event reconvened at Strings restaurant afterward for even more terrific food. Chef Noel Cunningham's waiters put together two long tables, and restaurant critic Pat Miller told everyone where to sit. It was generally understood that her decisions were final. Noel bounced up and down, serving platters straight from the grill as if we were in his home. Grant recipient Jim White of the Volunteers of America, who relied on this event for a substantial percentage of his annual budget, sat at the far end, leaning back in his chair and raising toasts as if the winning Power-ball lottery ticket were in his pocket. Everyone seemed extremely pleased.

I spent a good part of the evening talking with Leo Kiely, the president of Coors Brewing Co., a local sponsor of the event. Sometime after midnight and after a few martinis, he pulled a chair over, handed me a cigar, and said, "We get a lot out of this relationship. A lot!" He had an encyclopedic grasp of Coors' market share in each of fifty different cities and an intuitive feel for where they were poised to improve. "I'd love to hear your vision of where Share Our Strength is headed," he said, "and also challenge you to make us a bigger part of it." He reached into his pocket and handed me a little tool that snips the end off of cigars. Not realizing it was also a lighter, I proceeded to describe SOS's future, bragging about our distinctive sophistication in dealing with corporate partners, all while lighting the sleeve of my blue oxford-cloth shirt.

I also visited with others on the committee who had put weeks and months of personal time into everything from printing tickets and T-shirts to dealing with Coors Field's management. As at most Taste of the Nation events, the better part of the evening was dedicated to comparing crowd estimates and revisiting close calls, such as "Do you believe what time the forks showed up?"

A few of the veterans who have known me for a long time were disappointed that my late arrival prevented me from witnessing their success. At most events I attend, there is a short program in which I am introduced and make a few remarks, thank the sponsors and participants, and seek to give them some sense of the impact their efforts will have. But this night, I'd remained completely anonymous. Even among the small group of core organizers at Strings, most of those at the two tables were complete strangers to me and didn't know me or care. It's not the first time I've felt irrelevant at one of our own events, but it may be the first time being irrelevant turned out to be so instructive.

What we began years ago in Denver, and in so many other cities, is now institutionalized. In many cities, the event and the many ancillary activities—like press conferences and auctions—take place whether those at SOS headquarters do anything or not. That's not to say we can take it for granted. It's only because we never have taken it for granted that we enjoy the support and strength we do today. But we can take pride in the fact that thousands of people with no direct or personal connection to us now embrace as their own an event, an organization, and a cause.

SOS is decentralized by design. Within certain broad parameters, our local volunteers have wide latitude to shape and run their own efforts. The result has been a stronger organization. By empowering them, we have gained power. By relinquishing control, we have gained influence.

More important than the training or even the inspiration we've imparted is the new ambition we've instilled in them. We have not only created an organization that effectively serves others; we have created a cadre of stake-holders, a palace guard if you will, who care as much about preserving and expanding the organization as we do. When sociobiologists find this in ants or bees, they declare a higher order of evolutionary activity. Though this is the very essence of self-preservation for any species or institution, few organizations set out consciously to accomplish it. If they intend to grow and endure, then they must. There is nothing as difficult as this to accomplish, and nothing more important to guaranteeing lasting progress. What's been built through Share Our Strength is larger than any person or group of people, and it has been built to last.

III

When I was in sixth grade at Colfax Elementary School in Pittsburgh, I was put on the swim team by our phys-ed teacher, Ken McDonough, for the simple reason that he was also the lifeguard at our summer swim club where my parents, on hot days, bought him Cokes.

At Colfax we swam once a week in a small cloudy pool in the basement of the school. We wore thick navy-blue cloth bathing suits that could not have held more water if they were made of sponge. In a swim meet at the end of the season, I won the twenty-five-yard breast-stroke race.

Somehow, my time broke the city record, and the *Pittsburgh Post-Gazette* declared me the new record holder. This said more about the city's poor state of record keeping than my athletic ability. But as a result of the publicity, newspaper stories, and word of mouth regarding my unlikely feat, coaches throughout the county descended upon me and my parents. My future in competitive swimming seemed a foregone conclusion.

On this flawed premise, I swam competitively for the next six years. I took private lessons and often practiced three times a day. My coach entered me in hundreds of events throughout the tristate area. It proved to be an almost reckless waste of money and chlorine. I was an entirely mediocre swimmer. I never again enjoyed even one victory that approximated the fluke of my sixth-grade year. I trained with other swimmers who were far more competitive than I was; some legitimately had their sights set on the Olympics. It was obvious that I wouldn't be one of them. What was not obvious was how I got to be there in the first place. No one stopped to question the odds of a twenty-five-yard sprinter being transformed into Olympic material.

The task of building an institution to end poverty is Olympian in scale.

Our mission today requires dramatically different preparation, skills, resources, and strategies than anything the young Share Our Strength could have imagined during our successful sprint to fund emergency food assistance. Despite the fact that we've got Taste of the Nation events down to a science, the task of ensuring that people have enough to eat in this country is anything but simple. It's a long-distance race if ever there was one, requiring not only money and smart strategies, but the construction of new institutions. So if there are days when it seems like what we're trying to do is incredibly hard, confusing, and frustrating, and its outcome seems uncertain, it's because what we are trying to do *is* incredibly hard, confusing, and frustrating, and its outcome *is* uncertain.

What is certain is that we have much to learn from where we've come and much to learn from each other.

It is not easy to create an organization to work for social change, but what's even more difficult is sustaining and growing such an organization. Share Our Strength is now fifteen years old. Some of the very difficult challenges Share Our Strength has faced are precisely the challenges faced by other entrepreneurial organizations seeking to effect social change. They include budget constraints, staff turnover, the availability of top-flight talent, conflicting priorities, the need for management expertise, and the need to maintain both an internal and an external focus. They all occur in the context of addressing social problems larger than ever imagined or anticipated in the first place.

I've seen this not only firsthand at SOS, but also up close as a board member of other organizations like City Year's youth service corps, Community Impact!, and Echoing Green, the national fellowship program for social entrepreneurs. I've seen it as an adviser to Teach for America and Highway One. I've seen it in Community Wealth Ventures' clients ranging from the Enterprise Foundation to the Chicago Children's Choir.

Even more daunting is that these organizations are attempting to address social problems, like seemingly intractable inner-city poverty, that are so complicated and high-risk that the institutions originally set up to address them—government institutions—have pulled back if not given up entirely. For example, the Enterprise Foundation is trying to do for affordable housing what the Department of Housing and Urban Development is supposed to do, but Enterprise has just a fraction of the funds and staff.

How does an organization make the transition from its initial mission of delivering emergency services to the more complicated, politically charged, and long-term mission of changing underlying social conditions? How does an organization originally built on volunteers and sympathetic donors create wealth to become truly self-sustaining? How do you find, recruit, and retain the diverse professional talents necessary to build an enduring global institution? How does an organization extract lessons from its own best practices, build upon them, and make them available to others to leverage even greater change?

It's remarkable how many organizations and how many talented people are all stuck in the same place, wrestling with this same set of issues. Each has followed a similar trajectory, journeying across three phases of their work.

In their initial burst—the "lightbulb phase"—the founder or founders have an idea and are challenged to bring it to reality. They have to do all of the nuts-and-bolts things necessary to start a school, shelter, health clinic, or advocacy organization: write a mission statement, rent an office, form a board of directors, get their tax-exempt status approved by the IRS, and finally, organize a pilot project and begin to show results. Often, the idea is attractive because of its novelty, their enthusiasm, and the need it addresses. The founders dip into their own bank accounts, and family, friends, and a few "angel investors" provide the seed capital.

Having survived the start-up phase, an organization moves to the second level—the "low-hanging fruit" phase—in which the idea must be kept alive and sold to a broader audience. The first press clip is photocopied a thousand times and used like bait to get meetings, attract foundation dollars, impress supporters, and interest other media. Having proven that the idea works, the focus becomes replicating it in multiple sites. The founders sustain themselves by picking the rest of the "low-hanging fruit" and maybe expanding their program delivery into approximately ten other cities. Everything takes almost twice as long as expected, but it is worth it. The organization becomes known as a "cutting-edge" organization; money gets easier to raise, and quality staff is easier to attract. It is still small enough to be run without sophisticated management skills. The founders become well known in the community in which they work and are asked to participate on panels and make presentations at conferences.

The third phase is where many organizations find themselves today. The twin challenges at this level are expansion to scale and long-term sustainability. Their language is filled with abstractions like "crack the code" to get "to the next level," but what they are really trying to figure out is how to institutionalize, grow, and endure. In relative terms, there is financial stability. The organization no longer needs to worry about money to make payroll and survive, but now that the low-hanging fruit has all been picked, there is a shortage of money needed to grow. Although money is always helpful, money is just one of many obstacles. There is a severe shortage of top managerial talent. Many organizations at this stage are still being managed by their founders or by whoever has worked there longest, not necessarily by whoever the best available managers might be. Strategies for attacking the root causes of an issue are far more complicated than strategies for alleviating the symptoms, and therefore far less developed. Unlike the first two phases, they have neither the tools, training, or road map to get there. There are few mentors because, so far, few have achieved their third-phase goals, and those who have succeeded have not yet established a capacity for teaching others.

In June 1996, a group of businesspeople creating social-sector initiatives met with the management consultant Peter Drucker, honorary chair of the Peter F. Drucker Foundation for Nonprofit Management, whose mission is to lead social-sector organizations toward excellence in performance. In a letter, one of the participants, Bob

Buford, who chairs the board of Texas-based Buford Television, described Drucker's advice to the group: "You are not unique in what you are doing. There are many social entrepreneurs with great ideas, but so many don't survive. Many initiatives will not exist in one year, two years, or five years. What will make you unique is sustainability, the ability to develop and resource your organizations for growth and longevity."

Bob Buford considered his meeting with Drucker to be a turning point, after which "it became clear that what is needed is marketplace, business, and professional leaders/partners for these social entrepreneurs . . . to bring the skills learned in the marketplace to add value and build organizational capacity for the social-sector initiatives."

Drucker, Buford, and others have added immeasurable value to the nonprofit community by sharing their understanding of better management and business practices. They are right in advocating that nonprofits need to be run more like businesses. What is usually meant by that is simply that nonprofits must be run with professionalism. They should do what they are good at and not hang on sentimentally to things they'd like to do but have no core competency for. They should be accountable. They should measure impact. No one could argue with any of that, but those who embrace this "run-like-a-business" philosophy by itself are perpetuating a popular and misleading myth, which is that simply by adopting business practices nonprofits will be able to sustain themselves and last. Creating social change is not the same as creating shareholder wealth. Creating community wealth is not the same as creating shareholder wealth. The lessons of business are valuable, but they are in no way enough.

IV

Peter Goldmark recently left the presidency of the Rockefeller Foundation, one of the nation's largest charitable foundations, which makes grants to as many as nine hundred nonprofit organizations a year in a variety of fields ranging from arts and humanities to environment and economic development. He observed that "at this moment in history, we are more dependent on the nonprofit sector for ideas, innovation, and experimentation than any generation that has come before. The nation-state can't do it alone. *We are now challenged to be institution builders.*"

For Share Our Strength, this means our work is no longer just about feeding people, or even about addressing the root cause of hunger, which is poverty. Rather, our work is also about building a lasting institution to carry on such efforts over the long haul. That is something very different from where we began. It is an ambition that evolved over time, not one that anybody had the preparation or capacity to achieve at the outset. It requires different skills, resources, and strategies.

In practice, that translates into hiring people who not only excel at service delivery but also at managing others, designing organizational structures, and planning strategically. It means educating partners and donors about why only a portion of their dollars will go directly to the purchase of food. It means investing for the future and not just spending for today, and communicating to colleagues so that they understand why. Going forward, we must strike a delicate balance between honoring all of the great work we've already done and recognizing and admitting just how different is the necessary task of institution building that lies ahead.

In their book *Built to Last,* James Collins and Jerry Porras describe the characteristics of visionary companies that have demonstrated an ability to endure despite changing times and changing economic conditions. The book became a bestseller, fueled in part by an economy whose entrepreneurs and venture capitalists were starting record numbers of new companies, most of which aspired to thrive, grow, and last. The promise of immortality has always been seductive enough to find a wide audience.

The authors make the case that "visionary companies distinguish their timeless core values and enduring purpose (which should never change) from their operating practices and business strategies (which should be changing constantly in response to a changing world)."

For a time, *Built to Last* was required reading at SOS. It still should be. The specific methods of "preserving the core and stimulating progress," like the risk-taking involved in setting Big Hairy Audacious Goals (BHAGs), and "high levels of action and experimentation—often unplanned and undirected—that produce new and unexpected paths of progress," are clearly ingrained in our own distinct culture.

Built to Last has enjoyed more than forty printings and been translated into thirteen languages. The book's popularity spilled over into the nonprofit sector as well, which is how it came to our attention. But for all of its usefulness, *Built to Last* is fundamentally a book about, and for, corporations that create shareholder wealth. The needs of organizations like Share Our Strength that aspire to create social change are different and distinct. The *Built to Last* principles apply, but by themselves are insufficient. They offer a useful blueprint of a potential foundation but not the bricks and mortar of a lasting structure. That can't come from any corporation's experience. That can only come from our own experience.

There are only very rare examples in the nonprofit sector of visionary organizations that are built to last. Even the select few that have grown truly national—Boys and Girls Clubs, the Nature Conservancy, Big Brothers and Big Sisters—are strong more in relative terms, compared to other organizations, than in absolute terms.

Most nonprofits are initially inspired less by a desire to create an institution of social change than by a passionate personal interest in addressing a specific human problem that someone witnessed with his or her own eyes: A homeless person's recurring appearance on the corner becomes the catalyst for a local activist to start a shelter. A successful physician's chance encounter with children who lack immunizations and health care leads to the launch of a new child health organization. The tragic paralysis of a friend provides the motivation to create a new medical research foundation. Thousands of such organizations have been created to work in a specific community, on behalf of a specific objective, for a period of time. The founder's motivation is invariably to solve a particular problem, not necessarily to build a great organization for the sake of building a great organization. In many cases, whatever they've begun either dies out or plateaus at a certain level of activity.

The authors of *Built to Last* show us that in the corporate world, visionary and enduring institutions are founded from the opposite motivation. Starting with Bill Hewlett and Dave Packard's decision to start a company first and then figure out what they would make later, they conclude: "We had to shift from seeing the company as the vehicle for the products to seeing the products as the vehicle for the company." In advocating a shift in thinking "to seeing the company itself as the ultimate creation," they suggest that "the continual stream of great products and services from highly visionary companies stems from them being outstanding organizations, not the other way around."

Moving from theory to practice, this shift means "spending less of your time thinking about specific product lines and market strategies and spending more of your time thinking about organizational design." This is not something that has come naturally to Share Our Strength or to colleague organizations like the Food Research and Action Center, Kaboom, Children's Defense Fund, Food and

Friends, the Children's Health Fund, and many others. Many make the point that their goal is to go out of business, meaning that they hope that eventually the services they provide won't be needed. There are no circumstances in which the founder of a for-profit corporation would speak that way. Indeed, although meant jocularly, it reflects a mindset that is the opposite of the "built to last" mentality.

Ironically, our work, even when successful, is usually not institutionalized and does not grow to scale. This is true even when there is no decrease in demand or shortage of "customers" for the "product." Most organizations simply fail to reach all of those who need what they offer. Even more frustrating is the high likelihood that in time, another similarly intentioned organization will be created alongside it, will reinvent the wheel and experience the same futile organizational life cycle. This is true both because the motivations of nonprofit founders differ from corporate founders, and because traditionally a different set of economic laws have applied.

Though often overlooked, there are two specific reasons why even the most effective nonprofit organizations do not last, grow to scale, or reach as many people as they should.

The first reason why most social-change organizations don't last is that they didn't think they would need to. They did not aspire to last, and therefore they were not designed to last. Most community-based nonprofits were set up with the intention of filling what was perceived as a temporary gap. Hunger is a perfect example. The vast majority of community-based antihunger efforts that exist today were created in response to President Reagan's budget cuts in the mid-1980s. At the time, we thought of hunger as episodic, not chronic. When the economy faltered and unemployment was high, there seemed to be a tacit agreement that during the period when government had to cut back, private organizations had to step in temporarily, even though we could never do so on the needed scale.

Implicit in that agreement was the faith that when the economy recovered, government would resume some reduced but still significant role. Instead, years of pressure to reduce the size and expense of government culminated in federal law not only repealing welfare, but also repealing basic food assistance. Millions of single mothers and immigrants left welfare only to be plunged further into poverty. It reminds me of Mary Black's lyric "I thought you were saying good luck, but you were saying good-bye." No private nonprofit ever expected to fill a gap that large.

The second reason follows from the first. Since organizations didn't expect to be around for a long time, they didn't put in place any of the ingredients that would enable them to be around for a long time. Salaries, which in some cases were never envisioned in the first place, ended up being set low, making it impossible to sustain the development of a long-term team. Because becoming self-sustaining beyond foundation dollars was never envisioned, no steps were put in place to do so—no revenue-generating apparatus was created. Once an organization does establish an ambition of being built to last, it must backtrack and fill in all of these needs after the fact.

V

One of the indispensable ingredients of building cathedrals or lasting institutions is leadership. Nothing great and enduring gets built on its own. A vision, a sense of direction, and the relentless pressure to finish what has been started all come from a leader.

A cottage industry of courses and seminars to teach leadership development and leadership training flourishes today. The Institute for Leadership Development; Leadership Management Development Center, Inc.; the Centre for Leadership Excellence—you can find more than six hundred of them on the Internet, and that's not counting the considerable offerings of universities and the large international consulting firms like Arthur Andersen and KPMG Peat Marwick. Experts ranging from Peter Drucker to Stephen Covey lecture, teach, and consult on the topic.

Leadership has many definitions, and there are many kinds of leaders: political leaders, military leaders, business leaders, religious leaders, and, increasingly, citizen leaders. My own definition of leadership is a simple one built around the one thing they all have in common: getting people to a place they would not get to on their own.

It might be a philosophic place like free-market capitalism, or a political position like support for welfare reform. It might be a geographically literal place—Mt. Everest or the rain forest—or a personal place where individuals adopt and demonstrate new ethics and conduct.

Getting people to travel from one fixed point to another is what the work of leadership is about. If they could get there on their own, then no external force, leadership or otherwise, would be necessary. This definition of leadership comes with a very specific way of measuring results. The measure is the distance of the journey—whether they've made it and how far they've come.

It takes no leadership to get teachers to support higher teacher salaries or Sierra Club members to oppose the destruction of forests or national parks. They don't have to traverse any distance to arrive at such positions because these are the positions they're starting from in the first place. But it does take leadership to convert conservative business leaders into supporters of federally funded school lunch and breakfast programs, or to persuade financially stretched taxpayers to support funding for the arts.

If you accept the above definition of leadership as true, several other truths are inherent in it.

First, a leader will encounter resistance, some of it fierce at times. This is because of the reasons people do not reach a destination on their own in the first place. Either they don't want to, don't know how to, or are afraid to. Their discomfort will manifest itself as resistance. Leadership must anticipate and overcome resistance. Like a wise lawyer who builds a case not just on its strengths but by looking for holes in his own argument and preparing to rebut his adversary's every charge, a strong leader will try to see things from the point of view of those who disagree.

Moreover, the most effective leaders do not concentrate all of their energies on addressing and organizing those who agree with them, but rather on building bridges to those who disagree and winning them over to their point of view. Advocacy is not advocacy when aimed at those who share your views. That is redundancy. The key to solving most problems is in building a larger consensus than previously existed for a solution.

Next, assuming that the leader is leading because he or she got there first, then by definition there is a period in which the leader is alone. Initially, a leader may not have allies. Initially, a leader may not have others to either interpret, support, defend, or help sell his or her views. This may be lonely and isolating, but that is why leaders stand out from others.

Third, leadership is dynamic, not static. Once a leader gets people to a place they would not get to on their own, they must then be brought even farther. The horizon recedes with each step you take toward it. The nature of progress is not to rest or to accept the status quo. So the entire cycle begins anew. The irony is that the farther the distance a leader succeeds in bringing people, the farther they will feel from the safety of their home. They may be most resistant just when a leader feels they should be most ready to follow. They may be most skeptical just when they are the closest to their destination.

Finally, the leader who is ahead of the crowd either started there or had to pass people to get there. The people who were passed may not like that. Usually a deft touch is more effective than a sharp elbow. When I worked for Senator Gary Hart during his presidential campaigns, I'd watch how a Secret Service agent got to the front of a crowded room quickly. He didn't push. When someone is pushed, especially from behind, they push back or, at a minimum, brace themselves by planting feet and body more firmly. A well-trained Secret Service agent in a hurry will get through a crowd using the lightest possible touch—two fingers against a shoulder, the heel of the palm brushing the small of a back. You'd be amazed how readily people step aside and let you through.

Leaders are smart, but a leader need not be smarter than the people being led. In fact, that is rarely the case. Likewise, a leader need not be richer or have more resources. It is often said that leadership requires courage, vision, and strength, and that is probably true. But what leadership mostly requires is knowing where you want to go and staying faithful to that goal. A compass is a leader's most valuable tool, more so than brains or money.

Leaders employ a variety of tactics to move their followers. They give speeches, tell stories, make reasoned arguments, serve as examples, and conduct symbolic acts. All of these tactics are designed to do one thing: persuade. Persuasion is most successful when it shows how the recommended course of action is in one's self-interest. The intersection of self-interest and a larger public interest is where leaders stake their claim.

Cathedral builders were leaders. They were also entrepreneurs. "Entrepreneur" has become one of the most popular words in the vernacular today, invoked to describe almost any success in creating something new. The word means many different things to many different people. Entrepreneurs start things. They have passion. Other characteristics include innovation, youth, risk, and commitment. But these are what *characterize* an entrepreneur, not what defines one.

"Entrepreneur" is a very polite word, because what it really means is "rule breaker." Whether in the business sector or the social/public sector, that is the distinguishing characteristic of what entrepreneurs do: they break the rules. They do things their way, a new way, or whatever way necessary, rather than the defined way.

There's only one way to follow the rules, but many ways to break them. Entrepreneurs break rules by taking risks others would not take, by exposing themselves to greater potential loss than would others or, perhaps, than common sense dictates. Such rule-breaking is for a purpose, of course: The purpose is getting to a desired outcome. The ends justify the means for most entrepreneurs.

They break rules by using resources not as they were designed to be used, but however they are needed. Noel Cunningham uses a restaurant not just as a business, but as a headquarters for antihunger efforts. Gary Mulhair not only helped to rehabilitate ex-cons and make them employable, but used them as the labor in the highly profitable enterprise that funded their rehab. Entrepreneurs rearrange resources and use them in ways they never were used before.

Entrepreneurs seize opportunities even after plans have been painstakingly devised, agreed upon, and set that preclude them. They break rules by thinking outside of them, not because they are rebellious or ornery, but because their own lives have not followed a linear path. They bring experience and learnings from one sector and apply them to another.

Entrepreneurship has come to be so worshiped that some view it as an end in itself, but leaders are not entrepreneurs just for the sake of being entrepreneurs. Rather, they use entrepreneurship as a technique of their leadership.

CHAPTER SEVEN

Lessons of a Storyteller

I

You don't expect the people you fund or the children you feed to get shot and killed, but when you work in some of the most troubled neighborhoods in America, it happens far too frequently. It underscores the life-and-death nature of what's at stake in the struggle to improve conditions stubbornly resistant to change.

Usually, the letters I receive from Share Our Strength's grant recipients mention small triumphs or tribulations—the announcement that a major gift has been received or an endowment fund established, a progress report on the capital campaign, a favorable press clip circulated or a negative story rebutted. Letters like these come by the dozen every day, but when I hear from Geoffrey Canada, an SOS board member in Harlem who is one of the most respected child advocates in the country, I learn that something more immediate, more personal, indeed more vital is at stake.

Geoffrey is the president and CEO of the Rheedlen Centers for Children and Families. Rheedlen is designed to be a safe haven for inner-city children. It includes forty-three before-, during-, and after-school programs serving more than four thousand children from Harlem to Hell's Kitchen. It also runs a program called Peacemakers, which trains young people to literally keep the peace on playgrounds and in classrooms.

A safe haven is something most of us take for granted. Our homes are safe and so are the places where we work, learn, play, and shop. We don't need to create a special designation for a space that is safe. But the safety that is naturally ubiquitous in some neighborhoods is as hard to find as a needle in a haystack in others. Creating, preserving, and protecting that safe space often requires a concerted effort that would be unimaginable elsewhere.

In September 1997, Geoffrey wrote to break the news that Davidchen Joseph had been shot and killed. Davidchen had grown up at Rheedlen and made the center his home. Davidchen's twin brother had asked the wrong question at the wrong time to the wrong gang member. Two members of the gang pulled out handguns, and the twin brother ran. Davidchen was on his bicycle and unable to get away. He was shot dead on the spot.

Davidchen was twenty years old, went to school, and worked. He sang in his church choir and had a beautiful voice. Along with his two brothers and one sister, he had been raised by a single mom until her death five years before. Then, the children were on their own, and Geof-

frey began to work with them personally, treating Davidchen as his own son and making him part of the Peacemakers program.

Geoffrey has many sons, some biological and more he
just treats that way. He told me that Davidchen's death had
affected him deeply, and it affected me that way too. It's
one thing to experience reversals and disappointments in
your work, but the loss of a child is permanent. Tomorrow's success or victory can't make up for it.

I first met Geoffrey Canada where most people first meet
him: on the op-ed page of *The New York Times*. In 1992, the
newspaper published a speech that Canada gave to the Robin
Hood Foundation upon receiving its Hero's Award. The
headline was MONSTERS, and Canada began his remarks by
saying, "Some people might be a little more modest and say
'Don't call me a hero. I'm not worthy of such flattery.' But
not me. I desperately want to be a children's hero." He went
on to explain that children in New York City need heroes
because "heroes were meant to slay dragons and monsters,
and far too many of our children face monsters every day." It
was not the voice one usually finds on *The New York Times*'s op-
ed page. There was simplicity and directness, both seriousness and playfulness. What came through most clearly was
his courage to stand apart and his passion for getting others
to see what he has seen.

The children that Canada was speaking of are the children who grow up poor, hungry, and amid violence, like
the children he grew up with in the Bronx and now works
with in Harlem every day.

In the neighborhood where he works, 47 percent of the families live below the poverty line. There are 14,333 people who live there; 2,628 of them are children between the ages of five and seventeen. Geoffrey knows this because he counted them. Sixty-one percent of these children live in poverty. At the local elementary school, P.S. 207, fewer than 20 percent of the children read at or above grade level. Many fail the examinations required to graduate into middle school. Geoffrey believes "there is no way you're going to save a kid if you don't know him personally." Geoffrey Canada knows kids—personally. He's risked and dedicated his life to saving them, especially from violence.

It would be hard to find a more dramatic contrast between Geoffrey's neighborhood and the leafy campus of Bowdoin College in Maine where he received his bachelor of arts degree. It would be even harder to find any connection between Rheedlen's world and Bowdoin, except possibly for the fact that Harriet Beecher Stowe, whose book *Uncle Tom's Cabin* raised national awareness of the horrors of slavery and incited support of abolition, wrote most of her book in a study in Bowdoin's Appleton Hall. After Bowdoin, Canada got his master's at Harvard's Graduate School of Education.

Harlem may be a far cry from Harvard, but not from the South Bronx neighborhood where Canada grew up forty-seven years ago, and where he remembers "cooking potatoes in a hole in the ground in the backyard, which was really an empty lot behind our tenement." His alcoholic father abandoned him and three brothers when he was four years old. The combination of welfare and his mother's income was not always enough to pay the rent, so the family moved a number of times.

I went to visit Canada at his headquarters on Broadway near 107th Street, walking up three flights of stairs to get to his office. Inside, boxes, printers, and copiers filled the corridors, and the walls were mostly bare. It looked more like a temporary facility than a building they'd occupied for almost ten years.

Canada doesn't have a fancy office on the top floor because he doesn't need one. His work is at street level. He needs to be where the kids are, to know them by name and work with them directly. The goal is not to raise money for children's issues, or do advocacy for children's issues, or bring greater awareness to children's issues, although he does all of these. The goal is to be with the children who need him. As he wrote in his memoir *Fist Stick Knife Gun*:

> *This problem cannot be solved from afar. There is no way that government or social scientists or philanthropy can solve this problem with a media campaign or other safe solutions operating from a distance. There is no safe way to deal with the violence our children face. The only way we are going to make a difference is by placing well-trained and caring adults in the middle of what can only be called a free-fire zone in our poorest communities. Adults standing side by side with children in the war zones of America is the only way to turn this thing around.*

Canada met me in the reception area, looking fresh and trim in a suit tailored to his lean body. I extended my hand to shake, but he embraced me in a big hug instead, as gentle and expressive as a third-degree black belt in martial arts allows one to be. We walked back down the stairs and out onto the busy sidewalk to look for a restaurant where we could talk.

Canada has been at Rheedlen since 1983, when he became program director for their Truancy Prevention Program. In 1990, he was named president and CEO, taking over from Richard Murphy, whose legacy had been the development of the Beacon Schools Program, which redesigned schools to become multiservice centers open days and evenings, seven days a week, 365 days a year. The range of programs offered at the Beacon school includes aerobics, dance, adult education classes, and workshops in areas that parents choose. Social workers are on-site to provide individual intensive counseling.

It wasn't an easy beginning. In *Fist Stick Knife Gun*, Canada remembers the first time he looked at the site for the program:

> At first glance I saw the extreme poverty and felt the sense of desolation. The young men and teenagers hanging on the corner looked at us with open hostility, knowing that three black men with coats and ties had to be a threat of some kind. They thought we were either cops or maybe real estate speculators coming to displace more people from the neighborhood. The only adults visible were sitting not ten yards from

the entrance to the school, drinking beer and wine and not even bothering to hide the bottles. They too looked at us with suspicion. It was clear that to everyone on the block we were a momentary interruption in their existence, people with ties just passing through. This was a block that people who could afford to had long since fled, a block you can find in any city in America.

Canada considers the Beacon schools the most successful thing he's ever been involved with, and is quick to explain that a Beacon school "is more than just a bunch of services for children and families, it is a community-development strategy. We have realized that you cannot save children without saving their families, and you cannot save families without rebuilding communities. Beacon works on all of these issues at the same time."

Borrowing the schools and keeping them open to serve the community strengthened both. Rheedlen's ambition to capitalize on such an underutilized resource reminded me of the eagerness President Lincoln expressed when General George B. McClellan would not use the resources at his disposal to mount an attack. "If you're not going to use your army, I'd sure like to borrow it," Lincoln telegrammed him.

Every time I've reached out to Canada, I've found him a generous and patient teacher. He's not resentful, as he could be, of the outsider who can't imagine having to search for and build a safe haven or who has never been close enough to the ground to see the blood spill from a child. He does not give you the sense that he made a sacrifice by coming to Harlem, or that his own dream was deferred. He's fully aware how precious his own life experience can be to our nation's attempt to heal. What he wants most, as he told us, is to be the children's hero that he is.

II

Geoffrey Canada does something that Nancy Carstedt, Gary Mulhair, Noel Cunningham, and Alan Khazei do not do. He writes books. The first was about his own childhood and his work. The second book, published four years later, also by Beacon Press, is called *Reaching Up for Manhood* and is about transforming the lives of boys in America.

Over time, Canada's role at Rheedlen evolved from service provider to storyteller. It's a role vital to the cathedral-building strategy that makes social change last.

Geoff never thought of himself as an author, but from the time he was young he had a gift for communicating. "I remember when I was just thirteen, my mother looked at me and said, 'You've got something special in the way you talk to people, and I'm telling you right now that if you ever use it for evil I will never speak to you again.' So I always thought about how I should use it.

"Someone at Beacon Press approached me about writing a book. They were Marian Wright Edelman's publisher. I got my five-thousand-dollar advance and thought about it for a while, and then I said to my editor, 'So what is the way that you write a book?' She said, 'There is no certain way. You have to sit down and write it.' Well, I'd always kinda expected them to tell me how to do it. When I heard that, I was quite shook up. And I stayed shook up for a while."

Now, four years later, he's thought a lot about the importance of books, of storytelling, and how it advances the work.

"Books give you a longer time to talk to people than you would otherwise have," Canada told me. "It's a way of spending three or four or even six hours with someone. Think about it. Even your best friends who love you won't sit through six hours of listening about your work. I'm moved by the power of that.

"A second book is important in a different way than the first. People begin to take you seriously when they know they're going to be hearing from you again. It's a way of saying you're not going away, and of giving your ideas staying power.

"Books completely changed my life. *Manchild in the Promised Land*. That book just changed my life. I remember giving it to all my friends."

The power of stories should not be taken for granted. Canada is onto something that every leader needs to understand. Not everyone can or should write a book, but anyone dedicated to creating change must develop the capacity to share stories, ideas, best practices, and core values. The doctor and poet William Carlos Williams, speaking of his patients, once advised a student: "Their story, yours, mine—it's what we all carry with us on this trip we take, and we owe it to each other to respect our stories and learn from them."

Stories mark the tempo for civilization's slow but inexorable march forward, but they do more than that. Stories have power. The world changes when the ideas and beliefs of those who live in it change. This law of social-change dynamics is hardly a new one. Walk into a church or temple that is five or five hundred years old, and you instantly see that this storytelling is what the work is about. It is often one of the principle functions of the building itself. When the great cathedrals were built in the Middle Ages, 90 percent of the people alive at the time were illiterate. The stained-glass panels, the sculptures, the paintings and frescoes, all served the same purpose: They passed on the stories in a medium that was accessible and could be understood. The history, the values, the heroes and the villains, lessons learned the hard way, they are all right there. The guidebook for Washington National Cathedral explains: "A Gothic cathedral is meant to instruct as well as inspire. . . . The iconography of a cathedral is the system of images and symbols used in stained glass, sculpture, and other art to tell the Christian story." Sure enough, the varied artwork in Washington National Cathedral tells of everything from the stories of the Old Testament to the space program.

The community of progressive nonprofit organizations and public entrepreneurs is quite young and does not understand this. Most have struggled to survive. Some still do. There is always a concern that dollars spent on press, public relations, and communications might be better spent on direct delivery of human services. Storytelling could seem like a luxury. In fact, it is an absolute necessity if the learnings and practices of the community of public entrepreneurs and community-wealth builders are to survive from one generation to the next. Indeed, no species survives any other way. That's the role and purpose of the stories in this book.

Conservative think tanks and policy organizations have shown they do understand this. The National Committee for Responsive Philanthropy, whose mission is to make philanthropy more responsive to disenfranchised peoples, issued a report in 1997 about how conservative foundations had developed a coherent and strategic approach to philanthropy and public policy. It concluded that conservative foundations, such as the Heritage Foundation, the American Enterprise Institute for Public Policy Research, the Cato Institute, and others distinguished themselves by investing heavily and consistently in the communications capacities, marketing campaigns, and media outreach of the organizations they fund. They provide dollars not only for press and public relations, but for research and the publication of articles, op-eds, and books.

Many of the foundations studied engaged in such funding efforts for as long as two decades, which helped to ensure the financial stability of key conservative institutions, giving them a greater capacity to influence specific policies and audiences. They see storytelling and the role it plays in shaping public opinion as a strategic imperative. This was in marked contrast to the majority of foundations, which, according to the report, "tend to operate not with a long-term policy perspective but with a problem-oriented and field-specific approach. . . . Their commitments are short-term and project-driven, often looking for measurable outcomes rather than such vaguely definable goals as pushing public opinion in one direction or the other."

There are a lot of ways to tell stories, but one of the most effective is through books. Books accomplish three things:

First, they put your ideas in "pass-aroundable" form. A friend can tell another, "You've got to read this," hand her the book, and thereby transmit your ideas in exactly the way you've chosen. The genes are uncontaminated and the DNA unaltered. Your ideas get sold wholesale, not retail, and reach a much larger audience than you ever could personally.

Second, writing a book requires you to translate your ideas into a language accessible to others. The book you want to write may not be the book people want to read, and a good editor and publisher will help you make your book both of those.

Finally, a book creates a platform for discussing your work. It becomes a hook not only for book reviews but for radio and TV interviews, speech requests, and all types of public forums to discuss and further disseminate your ideas.

Making ideas and stories available this way is one of the fundamental obligations of leadership. Try to think of a leader—not just political leaders in the conventional sense of the word—who hasn't used storytelling to advance his or her goals. Name a single chef who has not put his or her ideas into a cookbook. Chefs use recipes not only to tell the story of their work but to perpetuate it. If their creations are to survive, others must know which ingredients are necessary and how to put those ingredients together.

Any individual or organization serious about creating lasting change must get serious about storytelling. This is not the same as public relations or getting good press. The storytelling needs to be strategic, and a capacity for the telling needs to be created just as surely as cathedrals create vehicles for telling the story of Christianity.

In his book *Extraordinary Minds,* psychologist and educator Howard Gardner, who introduced the idea of multiple intelligences, uses the example of Gandhi to argue that the major influencers (defined as "leaders") of their time relied heavily on storytelling. In contrast to most theories of leadership, which focus on the power of the leader or the policies that he or she pursues, Gardner believes "influence occurs significantly in a set of exchanges between the minds of leaders and the minds of followers. The principle vehicle of influence is the story; an Influencer achieves effectiveness by embodying in his or her life the story that he or she relates." He underscores that "a story is not merely a 'message' or a 'vision.' It is a full-fledged drama, one that grows naturally out of the life experiences of the Influencer, and one that seeks to envelop the audience in its own quest."

This turns out to be exactly what Geoffrey Canada did in his own writing, honestly chronicling the life of a once young inner-city child named Geoffrey Canada, his coming-of-age amid drugs, alcohol, sexual awareness, and violence. One *Boston Globe* columnist described him as "the brother who never left the 'hood because he keeps looking into the faces of the children and seeing himself there."

Storytelling is why we're here, according to Binx Bolling in Walker Percy's novel *The Moviegoer*. "There is only one thing I can do: listen to people, see how they stick themselves into the world, hand them along a ways in their dark journey and be handed along, for good and selfish reasons."

There is a need to create a formal capacity for getting the stories told. Just as the MacArthur Foundation uses nominators to award "genius" grants for which one cannot apply, there is a need for a foundation effort that will identify and support people who have stories to tell, people like Ashoka's founder Bill Drayton, Wendy Kopp from Teach for America, Nancy Carstedt at the Chicago Children's Choir, or Alan Khazei at City Year. Their stories are too important to leave it to chance that they'll have the time and resources to write books. The time and resources can be made available to them specifically for this purpose. Cash grants should be accompanied by technical assistance, agent representation, editing, and marketing support.

At the restaurant where we are having lunch, the proprietor greets Geoffrey Canada warmly, but he is not the only one who recognizes what Canada has achieved. He won the 1995 Heinz Foundation's prestigious $250,000 prize and the Parents Magazine Award. He hosted a PBS documentary on jobs and won the Governors Award for African-Americans of Distinction. Attorney General Janet Reno took it upon herself to come see his work.

When the check comes and we get ready to leave, I ask Geoff about his family and learn that he's just had a baby son, Geoffrey Jr. "It's so unfair," he says, and at first I'm not sure what he means. "My wife is home with him, and he is constantly being played with and talked to and has all this stimulation, which is what makes these kids grow up smart and strong, and there are so many other kids that are just left to sit somewhere. They're ignored. They grow up without any of what my son has. It's just so unfair."

I tell him about Zach and Mollie, what great kids they are, but how often they would be at a disadvantage if not for their parents intervening on their behalf in school, at their summer camp, with the neighbors. Children need to have an advocate, someone who coaches, counsels, defends, represents, and promotes them at all times. A caring parent is an advocate.

Canada agrees and says: "These kids need us the whole way. All of them. I don't care who they are: black, white, rich, poor. If you're a parent of a young teen and it's six o'clock at night and you don't know where he or she is, then you worry about them. And you should. If they turn out really wonderful, that doesn't necessarily mean we did a great job. And if they turn out troubled, that doesn't mean we did a terrible job. They are individuals."

CHAPTER EIGHT

You're Worth More Than You Think You Are

I

Cathedrals ain't cheap.

The truly beautiful cathedrals are the ones that get built, and that requires resources. Achieving the vision of change in your community will require creating new resources as well. Meaningful change is labor-intensive and takes time, often a lifetime. The organizations doing such work must think differently about themselves and how they will sustain themselves. Piety and good intentions can take you only so far. Where they leave off, money comes in.

When Dr. Benjamin Spock, the pediatrician and best-selling author, died in 1998, many of the articles and obituaries about him referred to the concise eight words of commonsense advice he offered to parents at the very beginning of his famous child-care manual: "You know more than you think you do." If Dr. Spock had set about to diagnose and prescribe for the millions of Americans working to improve their communities through volunteer and nonprofit activities today, he might well have begun with eight very similar words: "You're worth more than you think you are."

Community organizations and national nonprofits typically have more assets than they either appreciate or fully use. In fact, most have assets that would enable them not only to redistribute wealth but also to create wealth, a new kind of wealth called community wealth. Using assets in new ways to build revenue-generating enterprises through for-profit business enterprises can empower citizens and organizations across the country, yielding the resources necessary to increase the operating capacity of programs that work.

Whether or not they succeed in doing so depends on their ability to think in new ways about assets they may have previously taken for granted or not initially recognized as such. Fortunately, the best practices from the business world and the experiences of the most innovative pioneers in the nonprofit world have led to the development of specific processes that help organizations do just that. It all begins by believing and understanding that you are worth more than you think.

The creation of wealth and all it promises has forever been a seductive and powerful idea, a great motivator and enabler. It allows people to have things they need or want, and it gets things done. In its cause, continents have been opened, armies have been raised, and technologies developed at a pace once never imagined. Hopes and dreams have been built on its slightest hint and kept alive by its glitter, and they have been dashed and destroyed if built upon no more than that. Not surprisingly, its most vigorous advocates have been those who benefit most directly from the wealth being created.

Each generation, against the backdrop of its own time and opportunities, finds its way to create wealth. Until now, the tools and techniques may have varied, but not so the nature of the wealth itself. The Bill Gateses and Warren Buffetts of the world amass great fortunes, as did the Rockefellers and Carnegies, and in their wake millions of stock, bond, and mutual-fund investors, as well as others engaged in a growing economy, build nest eggs that reflect the smaller amounts of wealth created for themselves.

But today, community wealth is being created by social entrepreneurs and innovators drawing upon the most powerful incentives of the marketplace and bending them toward specific community purposes instead of personal enrichment. Like engineers rechanneling a river whose floods once lay waste to towns and villages in its path, these community-wealth builders are harnessing the best of what the market has to offer and using it to address community needs ranging from hunger and homelessness to environmental conservation and historic preservation.

The community-wealth movement is a radical departure from deeply ingrained practices that have constrained those working on behalf of the public interest to do so only with public dollars or private philanthropy. For some reason, they forfeited the marketplace long ago, simply walked off the field, or rather never walked onto it in the first place, and chose instead to settle for the crumbs instead of the cake, the very modest resources comprised of what's left over: what good neighbors, good corporate citizens, and wealthy families or foundations choose, at their sole discretion, to make available after all of their other more immediate and primary needs have been met. If the last thirty years have taught us anything about using charitable resources to meet pressing social needs, it is that you can't get there from here. The pool of charitable resources available in even the most generous society is still too shallow.

Nonprofit organizations typically fund their work through redistributed wealth, but some nonprofits are now beginning to take steps to create their own wealth. Some have already developed successful revenue generators like the licensing agreement for colorful ties that benefits Save the Children, or the brownies sold by Greystone Bakeries' formerly homeless employees that are now used in Ben & Jerry's ice cream. In Washington, the nonprofit D.C. Central Kitchen supports its perishable food rescue program by catering receptions, parties, and conferences for a fee. Although the dollars earned may cover only a portion of each organization's annual budget, they are valuable nevertheless.

On 122nd Street in Harlem, a youth development organization called Harlem Textile Works offers art education, job training, and employment to artistically talented but economically disadvantaged youth. Founded in 1984,

Harlem Textile Works generates nearly three quarters of its operating expenses through the sale of artwork, hand-printed textiles, as well as through design licensing which has included sales to Hallmark Cards. It is based on a vision of how talented young people can escape the streets of Harlem, not through the charity of others, but through their own unique talents, when those talents are aimed in the direction of creating self-sustaining profits.

In Richmond, California, Rubicon Programs, Inc., is a nonprofit community agency that serves economically disadvantaged, homeless, and mentally ill people. The organization's business ventures, which include a gourmet bakery as well as landscaping and janitorial services, have generated $3 million in annual revenues to support operation costs. Executive director Rick Aubrey stresses the importance of producing the best possible product: "People don't buy from us because we're the nicest nonprofit in the dessert case. They buy cakes from us because it's the best cake that's there. People like what we do, but they are not going to buy the cakes because of that. People want value in the products they get. They want service from us. Our salespeople are nicer. Our delivery is better. And, oh, by the way, we happen to be doing a good thing."

There are plenty of others who want to follow in these footsteps. The affluent community of Bloomfield Hills, Michigan, has one of the wealthiest school districts in the country, serving 5,700 students with an annual budget of $73 million. But tax cuts have slowed the growth of its academic program, and school district superintendent Gary

Doyle is convening workshops on how to generate additional dollars. "When we switched our thinking from the philanthropy of foundations to the development of goods and services through an Office of Enterprise, it was like a breakthrough, a paradigm shift." He believes that the expertise Bloomfield Hills developed in building a community-service curriculum might be marketable to other school districts. If he can raise between $1 million and $1.5 million in additional revenues, beyond what taxes bring in, he can keep the school district growing.

Likewise, Dave Blanchard, chairman of the board of Bancroft, Inc., a $67-million-a-year residential treatment program in New Jersey for severely developmentally disabled children and adults, anticipates a dramatic decrease in the government support they've always relied upon. Blanchard hopes to identify profitable opportunities based on the medical staff's state-of-the-art practices in brain trauma, autism, and other areas. Blanchard's stake in creating community wealth is more personal than most. His sister, who has already been at Bancroft for thirty years, will live out her entire life there. Her future depends on Bancroft moving toward financial self-sufficiency. "You can't make your own choices unless you're financially independent. I don't want my sister to live in a place run any other way."

The primary imperative behind creating community wealth is that America's social needs are outpacing the public and private dollars available to them. Total private giving in constant dollars grew extremely slowly from

1990 to 1994, and is projected to grow at an extremely slow rate—2 to 3 percent—through 2002. State governments are increasingly working to control costs as they become responsible for managing welfare programs without federal oversight. Under the president's budget plan, from fiscal year 1997 to 2002, nonprofit organizations would lose more than $40 billion of their federal revenues. Private giving would have to increase more than three times the current rate just to make up for the recently enacted spending cuts.

Charity is a valuable tool. It represents the best of the American character. But charity is not going to be enough. Redistributing wealth is another valid response. Compelling arguments can be made about why that would be fair and just in a prosperous America, but redistributing wealth is not going to be enough. Creating new wealth is the only answer for nonprofits and community-based organizations struggling to meet social needs.

Creating community wealth resonates in these waning days of the twentieth century, because we find ourselves at a unique historical junction. On the one hand, social policy is changing more profoundly than at any time in the last fifty years. Government programs that have been relied upon for feeding, housing, educating, and helping people in need are shrinking, being repealed, and most often not being replaced. At the same time, as best exemplified in a *Business Week* headline about Silicon Valley that read EVEN THE RECEPTIONISTS ARE MILLIONAIRES, wealth is being created at a pace, magnitude, and scale that is all but unprecedented in our lifetime. Low inflation, low unemployment, and stable interest rates have fueled sustained economic growth, but it is still an economy in which the gap between the richest and poorest grows wider, not narrower, and the economic boom fails to reach those who are in greatest need and the organizations that work with them.

Taken together, these two historic trends suggest a clear and compelling conclusion: It is incumbent upon those of us in service not just to work harder or raise more money, but to fundamentally rethink how we achieve our mission and the structures we've put in place to do so. Our response must be to commit ourselves not only to redistributing wealth, but to creating a new kind of community wealth. The most often repeated cliché in the antihunger field is that it is fine to give a man a fish, but even better to teach him to fish. Given the scale of the hunger problem, even that well-intentioned cliché may be a bit outmoded. What we really need to do is show those serving hungry people how to build fisheries.

This is what is at stake in creating community wealth: It will determine whether we address our most pressing social needs with whatever leftover resources are available, or instead with the best resources available; it will determine whether our progress is incremental or monumental; it will determine whether our grant recipients and community partners have the ability to do not only what is popular, but what is right; it will determine whether our grant recipients and community partners have the freedom to invest in themselves and their own operating capacity;

and it will determine whether those who live in and work closest to the communities they serve have the freedom to run their programs their way. For these reasons, community wealth means something far more important than money. It means dignity.

Kurt Vonnegut once wrote, "There is no reason goodness cannot triumph over evil, so long as the angels are as organized as the Mafia." There are angels at work all across America today. They are feeding, teaching, tutoring, mentoring, healing, and serving others. But they are not as organized as they need to be. They don't have the tools, training, and resources they need to fulfill their missions and achieve their potential. Community wealth can give them that.

II

The New Yorker magazine once published a cartoon in an issue just before the April 15 tax-filing deadline. A small boy, about six or seven years old, is sitting across the desk from an IRS employee, explaining: "Five percent of my income is from lemonade, and the rest is from charity."

Many nonprofit directors, probably most, could make a similar claim. They are almost wholly dependent on charitable contributions to support their very existence. That is always a frustrating position to be in, but never more so than in a prosperous economy when a vast amount of wealth is being created and is readily available for conspicuous consumption but not accessible to those working to address social issues.

A great paradox at the end of the twentieth century is that America's social institutions are undergoing profound change at the same time that wealth is being created at nearly unprecedented levels. Many of the safety-net programs that have long been relied upon to feed, aid, and comfort those most in need are being diminished if not entirely deconstructed, just at a time when society could best afford to support them. Sometimes, this paradox reveals itself in contrasts too glaring to ignore. On an airplane one morning in October 1997, I had *The Wall Street Journal* and a *USA Today* on my lap. In the second section of the *Journal,* I came across these six headlines on consecutive pages, which I recorded verbatim:

BUILDING-PRODUCTS COMPANIES EXPECTED TO POST
STRONG PROFITS FOR THIRD PERIOD

ON-LINE BROKERS ARE EXPECTED TO POST STRONG
RESULTS, BUT PRICE WARS LOOM

INSURERS TO POST ROBUST RESULTS FOR 3RD PERIOD

TRUCKERS TO POST STRONG THIRD QUARTER ON
HEALTHY FREIGHT LEVELS, UPS STRIKE

OIL-SERVICES FIRMS, ESPECIALLY DRILLERS, ARE EXPECTED
TO POST VERY STRONG RESULTS

OIL COMPANIES TO POST ABOUT 10% RISE IN PROFITS

As if to underscore the paradox described above, the same day's edition of *USA Today* had this headline: FOOD BANKS RUNNING ON EMPTY.

The point seems impossible to miss. Wealth is being created faster, in greater abundance, and is reaching more people than at any time in American history. But the vast majority of nonprofit organizations have been left behind. As they continue to experience drought despite the overflow of a booming economy, the time has arrived to consider a radical and less obvious proposition: It's their own fault.

I say this from the vantage point of one who has spent the better part of the last two decades laboring to reduce hunger and poverty in partnership and direct collaboration with nearly a thousand national and community-based nonprofit organizations across the country. The overwhelming majority are wed to practices that rely on redistributing wealth, rather than committed to the entrepreneurial activities that create wealth. The same is true for organizations dealing with education, health care, the arts, the environment, crime, domestic violence, and a host of other issues.

The notion behind nonprofits creating wealth sounds like a novel one, but it's actually something we learn even at an early age. I realized one night, while playing Monopoly at the kitchen table with my twelve-year-old son and eight-year-old daughter, that they had already figured out that it is better to own hotels on Boardwalk and Park Place than simply to wait to pass Go to collect $200. But not everyone in the nonprofit community has heard this message yet. Why haven't nonprofits learned this yet? How did the idea of bringing the world to your doorstep by building a better mousetrap become the exclusive preserve of the for-profit sector? What follows are specific suggestions on how to begin creating community wealth.

Repeat After Me: "Profit Is Good"

For some organizations, creating wealth will be an acquired taste. Jed Emerson manages the Roberts Enterprise Development Fund headquartered in San Francisco. George Roberts, principal partner in the leveraged buyout firm of Kohlberg Kravis Roberts & Co., established the fund to help Bay Area nonprofits generate revenues to become self-sustaining. Jed begins workshops for nonprofits by directing, "Repeat after me: profit . . . is . . . good." Jed says this because he needs to. Not everyone is there yet. The idea of making a profit and the things that need to be done to make a profit create discomfort for some nonprofit staffs. It's a threshold issue that any organization must address before it goes forward.

Because of the culture of nonprofits, and perhaps even because of the politics of the people who work in them, market forces are often viewed more with skepticism than with welcome, and for good reason. It is both the excesses of capitalism and the gaps that exist in a free-market economy that have left many people behind in our country.

After all, thirty million Americans live below the poverty line. We have all the proof we need that the market alone is not enough.

But market forces, if understood properly and used with discrimination, can also work to a nonprofit's advantage. Writing in *The Wall Street Journal* in January 1998, historian Arthur Schlesinger, Jr., declared: "The free market is unquestionably the supreme engine of innovation, production, distribution, and profit." Market forces cannot only be marshaled to generate revenues, but they can create incentives for an organization to reach a wider audience and create better products and services that make it more competitive for public attention and support. Market forces bring into stark relief the true costs and benefits of various activities and give managers more information with which to make decisions.

Housing Works is an organization started in New York in 1990 by AIDS activists committed to providing quality housing, health care, and support services to people living with AIDS and HIV in New York. Through the operation of thrift shops and a used-book café, the organization provides job training and employment to its clients while also generating revenue for Housing Works' operational costs. Executive director Charles King explains: "In our entrepreneurial ventures we are very much profit-driven. While our business enterprises have generally been aligned with our core mission, we also believe in creating a premium product for a premium price. If I can get my customers to pay high dollar, I get high profits, and I can pay high wages.

In fact, we're proud to say that we run the most expensive thrift stores in New York City and have the highest profit margins."

Typically, those who excel at creating and maintaining businesses are not very good at delivering social services, and vice versa, but they don't need to be. Two very different skill sets and life experiences are involved. You don't need to try to find someone with a joint master's degree in business and social work. You just need to create an organization where both kinds of people reside under the same roof.

The nonprofit and the for-profit sectors alike will have to cross a cultural divide if the community-wealth notion is to thrive. Many nonprofit groups think "profit" is a dirty word, while many businesses can't fathom how anything branded "nonprofit" can help improve their bottom lines. Both sides must become fluent in each other's language and enlightened about each other's values in the difficult task of strengthening our communities.

Howdy, Partner

Nonprofits don't understand the concept of partnership the same way businesses do. As someone who has been a grant-maker for the last thirteen years, I know that when a grant recipient comes to my office and explains that they don't want to be just a grant recipient, but that they instead want to be a partner, it can mean only one thing: They want to get an even bigger grant. There is really nothing "partnerlike" about it.

The idea of partnership is much in vogue today, because "partner" implies that mutual benefits are to be enjoyed by both parties, that they are on somewhat of an equal footing. But the definition of a grant-making relationship is that one is giving and the other is taking. There is rarely any talk about what would be offered in return. There is no clear sense of how both sides benefit, and that's okay, because the nature of the relationship is for benefits to flow just the one way. "Partnership" is not the right word for it.

When two businesspeople sit down together, they both need to gain something from the transaction they are discussing. What they gain must be tangible; they both need to be enriched. It is not good enough for one of them to get something and the other to simply feel good for having given it to him. This is so implicit that it is never said, nor does it need to be said. On the other hand, when a nonprofit sits down with a business, what is usually implicit in their sitting down, but not necessarily said, is "What we are doing as a nonprofit is so important and righteous that you should give us what it took you most of the past year to earn." This is an entirely different conversation and one that is not as sustainable over time.

Nonprofits and businesses *can* embark on partnerships that have real meaning and value to both. Understanding that you must have something concrete to give your partner is an important first step. Understanding how to discover and identify that "something" is the critical next step. *The touchstone of partnership is an understanding of the business needs and the self-interest of your potential partner.* This understanding can come about only one way: by asking. Never assume you know what a partner is trying to achieve until that partner has told you.

Our experience has been that the best way to build long-term, sustainable partnerships with companies like American Express, Evian, Barnes & Noble, and Calphalon is not by inundating them with information about hunger and persuasive arguments about why they should do more, but rather investing the time at their offices to learn about their sales and marketing targets, employee morale issues, public relations challenges, new product roll-outs, etc.

Businesses are not always prepared at first to respond to such questions from a nonprofit. Since their previous experience was probably with nonprofits asking for charitable "gifts," they won't understand why you need to know about business objectives and what you plan to do with such information. This must be explained explicitly. If you are successful, your counterparts at the company won't be in the position of going to their supervisors to ask for money to give away, but rather in the much stronger position of asking for additional resources that they believe will further specific business objectives of the company.

Stop Sitting on Your Assets

One of the most common methods of creating a revenue-generating opportunity for a nonprofit, whether in the area of licensing, cause-related marketing, or business enterprise, is to build such an opportunity on the foundation of already existing assets. Many organizations have assets beyond their ability to fulfill their mission, assets that they may have never considered as such.

The first step for any nonprofit is to consider whether they have, and perhaps have always had, an asset that they simply never considered as such, and whether it can be used to generate revenues. "Is there an asset we've created but never recognized as such that could translate into value in the marketplace?"

One great example is National Public Radio's popular program *Fresh Air,* on which authors are interviewed every evening. The demographics of who listens to *Fresh Air* are a publisher's dream: The people who listen are those who go out and buy the books they heard discussed. Next to being on *The Oprah Winfrey Show,* there isn't much that sells books as effectively as an appearance on *Fresh Air.* But who does it sell them for? Barnes & Noble, Borders, and the other large commercial bookselling chains.

Fresh Air, struggling to stay on the air in a competitive public broadcasting environment, came to recognize that it had an asset that it was essentially forfeiting to commercial booksellers. It recaptured that asset through a direct-marketing program that enabled listeners to call an 800 number, buy a book at a discount, and have it delivered to their home the next day.

Smaller organizations can succeed at this too. In Washington, D.C., the D.C. Central Kitchen recognized that its relationship with chefs and caterers, and the kitchen facilities it owned, were assets that it could leverage into a catering sideline.

One way to think about this is to pretend, for the purposes of the exercise, that your mission is going to be achieved by someone else for a time, and that a prominent local business leader has acquired your organization. She has asked you for a complete inventory of assets that might be deployed for business purposes, and since you don't have to think about the mission for even a second, you can concentrate on developing the most expansive list of assets possible.

Let's define assets as Things You Have + Things You Do: the three to four capabilities that can be leveraged to create community wealth.

Things You Have can include physical assets like the trucks of the hunger organization City Harvest, or the location and space of an institution like The Smithsonian Institute. It can also include access to desired resources or special relationships.

Things You Do might include being a low-cost producer, information manager, or developer of an innovative technique like the Compass School's methods for dealing with special-needs kids.

Other assets might consist of:

— access to celebrities
— large membership
— high-quality mailing list

— access to a low-cost workforce ·
— knowledge of and credibility in local communities
  and neighborhoods
— an easily identifiable logo

Mission Impossible

Whenever the American military confronts the pros and
cons of a possible deployment, such as recent missions in
Bosnia, Haiti, the Persian Gulf, and Somalia, one of their
biggest fears is "mission creep." The military defines "mission creep" as the escalation of the force's goals and responsibilities that can lead to an even more dangerous
circumstance, duties that not only expand but interfere
with and contradict one another. What begins as an effort
to remove chemical weapons capacity can evolve into a
peacekeeping mission, monitoring elections, capturing war
criminals, adventure. The military actively guards against
such mission creep because it decreases the likelihood
of doing any one thing well and increases the likelihood of
wasted resources and overall failure.

Nonprofits trying to create community wealth have not
yet learned this lesson. Indeed, they often do just the
opposite, loading themselves up with multiple missions,
failing to achieve clarity of purpose at the outset. There are
many sad stories in this regard, but to borrow a title from
the great novelist Carson McCullers, I'd put "The Ballad of
the Sad Café" at the top of the list.

An antihunger organization in New York had the arguably good idea to try to create a restaurant that would use its profits to support antihunger efforts. It was to be called One City Café. So far, so good. Then the organization decided that its restaurant should accept both dollars and food stamps. It turns out that in addition to raising revenues, the group's mission included providing a place where people on food stamps could receive a restaurant meal with dignity. Nothing wrong with that all by itself, but now the entire character of the restaurant has been changed, and by definition, it will be attracting a different clientele and creating a different set of profit/loss numbers. It turns out that the organization's mission also included job training for disadvantaged individuals who were transitionally homeless. And so it was felt that giving training to these individuals and placing them in positions as waiters would also be appropriate to the overall concept.

This is a prime example of mission creep run rampant. If any prominent restaurateur in New York—Danny Meyer from Union Square Cafe or Jean-Georges Vongerichten—opened a new restaurant, it would be at least a year or two before it was profitable, and that would be assuming the restaurant had everything favorable going for it. So to think of beginning with every possible disadvantage (or let's say "challenge," to be more politically correct) suggests an absence of clarity of purpose from the outset, at least with regard to the nonprofit enterprise.

One City Café closed its doors a little more than a year after opening. No profits were created for antihunger efforts. There is no restaurant where people on food stamps can eat. There is no job training at that site for people who are in transitional housing.

There is another way to go about it. What One City Café could have done was begin by building the best restaurant possible, giving itself every advantage, creating the best climate, and hiring the strongest possible staff. And then, after the restaurant became profitable, and only after the restaurant became profitable, other risks could be absorbed and other expenses incurred, such as the expense of training formerly homeless men.

Jim Collins, the coauthor of *Built to Last,* addressed this very issue in an *Inc.* magazine column comparing the social activism of Patagonia and Marriott. Patagonia has a long history of environmental activism, and Marriott, more conservative by nature, has launched a welfare-to-work program called "Pathways to Independence."

After describing the profound political and stylistic differences between the two companies, he concluded that they share two paradoxical traits: "Both see the corporation as a powerful tool for social change, and both have a ferocious dedication to profit." Collins admits that he "expected this from Marriott but not from Patagonia. Yet during a short tour of Patagonia's new surfboard start-up, [Patagonia CEO Yvon] Chouinard spent as much time talking about the importance and mechanics of profit as the need for social change. Patagonia might be a social vehicle, but it runs on an economic engine. It's not a question of social good or business profit, but social good *and* business profit."

Collins also describes a period of economic difficulties that each company experienced in the early 1990s and warns: "Had the two companies continued to decline, their social agendas would have become meaningless. Would anyone pay attention to a bankrupt Patagonia? . . . To do social good you must first and foremost perform well."

When revenue generation is the principal mission of a community-wealth enterprise, it is important to be clear about it. This might mean that the enterprise is not necessarily related to the mission of the organization, but there is no need to be shy or apologetic about this. Phil Collyer is the executive director of Greater D.C. Cares, which recently created a community-wealth enterprise of its own. He speaks compellingly of the need to be clear about mission: "Contrary to most nonprofits who have for-profit ventures, we are completely going away from the model in that we are starting a for-profit venture that has nothing to do with our mission. It's not antithetical to our mission— it's not a video store. It is placing attorneys in situations where they can act as temporary employees, and so, that is not an altogether different field from placing volunteers."

Greater D.C. Cares had clarity of purpose. They made a conscious decision not to be constrained by their mission, but to start a business that was going to make money, period. They looked at opportunities completely outside of their field—like reselling electricity, because the power utility field has just been deregulated—before settling on the legal temp business they call Cares@law.

Don't Try This at Home

The most common response of nonprofits after being introduced to the community-wealth concept is to say, "I understand what you're saying; I know it is what we should be doing and I want to get there, but we don't think that way or talk that way, and we need someone to come and help us do this."

Just because a nonprofit organization needs to move in the community-wealth direction doesn't mean it needs to try to get there by itself. There are several organizations that provide consulting or technical assistance in this specific area. They can be helpful in persuading a board to support community-wealth concepts, in assessing organizational capacity for going forward, and in training staff how to design and build community-wealth enterprises.

There are now a handful of efforts underway to help nonprofits create community wealth.

III

Our experience at Share Our Strength changed dramatically after the publication of *Revolution of the Heart*. I was accustomed to people coming up to me at an event or after a speech to ask how they could get a grant from SOS. That is the universal experience of grant-makers. But after the community-wealth concept gained currency, the most common request was not for money, but for technical assistance. "Would it be possible to have someone from the SOS staff consult to our organization or come and train us to build the kinds of partnerships that you've built?" Non-profits were beginning to think about how they could better leverage their assets to create new community wealth. It took a remarkably long time for it to click with me that SOS had an asset of our own which could be leveraged—our expertise.

We created Community Wealth Ventures to work with nonprofit organizations to identify and assess their assets in order to help them move beyond traditional fund-raising and design revenue-generating activities, including business ventures, partnerships, and licensing agreements.

Community Wealth Ventures is a for-profit subsidiary of Share Our Strength. It is conceived of more as an engineering and construction firm than a consulting firm, because its mission is to actually *design and build* community-wealth enterprises. We began this new venture for one simple reason: Our commitment to social change demands and depends on creating new resources to support those programs that are already proven to work but don't have the capacity to grow to scale. Helping others to design and build successful revenue-generating enterprises is the fastest way to advance the community-wealth concept.

But how could we make such services sustainable? The

organizations we most wanted to help were so poor that they were the ones least able to afford us (which is why we wanted to help!). It soon became clear, however, that there was a significant corporate market for such services. The nation's leading companies have retained Community Wealth Ventures for one of several purposes:

- to reorient their own philanthropy toward supporting nonprofits that are creating community wealth.
- to consult to their own grant recipients, so that those grant recipients would not be forever dependent on them. Some see the community-wealth concept as a corporate foundation exit strategy. Typically, corporate and other foundations fund an organization for three to five years and then must worry about whether the organization or its programs will be able to survive once such funding ends. Making the assistance of Community Wealth Ventures available to grant recipients is a way of adding value to grant partners beyond the dollars donated, and increasing the likelihood that they will be able to stand on their own.
- to explore whether the company itself can generate health and profit through its philanthropy.

And so we became our own first client, experiencing firsthand what an organization must go through to create a for-profit subsidiary, struggling with issues of talent recruitment, salary disparity, business develop-

ment, taxes and regulations, and capitalization. One extremely valuable early lesson was that capital exists to
begin such enterprises, if indeed they are structured as
business enterprises.

We concluded that we would need an initial, up-front
infusion of $600,000 to support Community Wealth Ven-
tures until our revenues and cash flow were at a level to
sustain our business. The five individuals I spoke to were
supporters of Share Our Strength, but not one of them had
ever donated more than $1,000 a year. Between the five of
them we raised the $600,000 in just a few weeks. It was
the shortest conversation I've ever had with any of them,
because it was a business they were putting their money
into. They liked the idea of investing in an effort that would
be run like a business, and that would recycle their money
back to them like a business investment. They felt like their
money was going to have a social impact, which was a big
part of their interest, but they were also going to get it
back, so that it could have a second social impact somewhere else if they so chose. Investments are risky; there
was no guarantee they would get their money back, but
compared to making a grant, in which the guarantee is that
they will not get even one penny back, this was a risk they
were willing to take.

The work of Community Wealth Ventures could probably have been accomplished just by creating another
department of Share Our Strength, but we thought there
were compelling reasons to approach this from a for-profit
perspective. First of all, we wanted to practice what we

preach. Our expertise is an asset to be deployed. More persuasive was the belief that market forces would result in better products and services, products and services that were really needed, as opposed to those that we thought would be good for others and that we would end up subsidizing.

There is a basic methodology that any organization can pursue to position and prepare itself for creating community wealth:

- Conduct an asset review. Identify the assets of the organization that will most contribute to an enterprise and any gaps that may influence the type of businesses considered. It is also necessary to develop a framework to assess the organization's strength in delivering upon each asset, as well as its position vis-à-vis other providers in the marketplace.
- Review options. Establish criteria for revenue generation and identify business opportunities that would match the needs and capabilities of the organization.
- Prioritize opportunities. Recommend enterprise ideas (businesses and/or corporate partners) meriting intensive development.
- Conduct high-level feasibility. Examine cost/benefit trade-offs, screen the ideas for viability, and eliminate those with insufficient revenue and/or excessive costs/difficulty of implementation.

Once a concept has been identified, the development phase begins. The basic activities for building an enterprise are:

1. *Market research* is designed to answer the overall question of whether there is demand for what you are offering. In addition, the data derived here will form the basis of your pro forma financial statements (which go into the business plan). Specifically, the research will answer such questions as:

— What products or services should you offer?
— What are the size, growth, tendency, etc., of the markets?
— Who is the target audience? How much would they potentially pay?
— Who else is offering these products and services? How are you distinct from these "competitors"? What are your strengths and weaknesses relative to competitors?

2. The *feasibility phase* will examine several things, but mainly:

— Organizational capacity and structure: What professional skills are needed, such as management, industry expertise, public relations, marketing, etc.? Are these skills available among staff and board members, or will they need to be contracted out or acquired? How many people need to be added?

— Potential profit and financing needs: How much income can you earn? What is the financial risk? How much start-up capital is required? How much is required to cover monthly operating costs and cash flow?
— Other issues such as the timing of the product/service offering, consideration of how the venture may affect your public image, etc.
— Do business opportunities fit within identified criteria (revenue, employment, types of employment opportunities created)?

3. The *business plan* will serve as the main tool to assist in attracting financing for the venture, but will also serve as a plan of action for its first few years of operation. An operational model for the enterprise is developed in this phase.

4. Deciding on *structure and financing* will be largely dependent on the results of the above analysis. Nonetheless, you can begin to consider different options and financing sources early on so that you will be ready to act as soon as possible.

Upon completion of the development process, you will have a feasibility study with an economic model, operational plan, and market-entry approach. These tools will be utilized to make a go/no-go decision and to seek financing of the enterprise, if appropriate.

Other organizations with assistance goals similar to Community Wealth Ventures include:

— The National Center for Social Entrepreneurs
— The Center for Nonprofit Enterprise
— The Roberts Enterprise Development Fund

Creating community wealth can revolutionize nonprofit work, community involvement, and citizenship by making substantial new resources available for social initiatives. The types of entreprenurial activities described above may not be for everybody or for every organization, but they *are* for a lot more organizations than are doing it now.

The challenge now is to strategically advance the concept. That will require:

— a clearinghouse of best practices
— technical assistance to nonprofits on everything from how to assess their own assets—or create them if necessary—to tax law and financial planning
— venture capital

It will also take a commitment by the business community to develop its own agenda for creating community wealth by joint venturing, sharing its skills, and supporting community-wealth enterprises through procurement of their products and services if they are competitive in terms of price, quality, and value.

In 1924, George Baker, the president of the First National Bank of New York, donated $5 million to build the campus of Harvard's Business School on the Boston side of the Charles River. Three years later, as construction was completed, the library was named for George Baker, and the administration building for his close friend and partner, J. P. Morgan. Next to John D. Rockefeller, Morgan is arguably the greatest symbol of capitalism and wealth creation in American history. Today, Morgan Hall houses the office of professor James Austin, whose job it is to challenge, train, and shape the minds of the elite nine hundred students admitted to the MBA program each year from among eight thousand who apply representing sixty-two countries.

The case method is the centerpiece of the school's method of instruction, and one of the cases Jim Austin teaches is the story of Share Our Strength and Community Wealth Ventures. Ultimately, community-wealth enterprises will grow and thrive when they are able to attract the best business minds and talent available. The challenge today is to ensure that students from the business, law, and professional schools at Harvard, Stanford, and other great universities don't view working in this sector as a career detour, but rather as a career builder.

CHAPTER NINE

Passion Rules the Universe

I

At age twenty-six, Mara Manus was the youngest female vice president for production in the history of Universal Pictures. She was also the first to fall off a horse and break her back in three places. The month she spent in bed and in a mobile cast proved to be a turning point. Not because it led to some sudden epiphany, but because it gave her the one thing that had been absent from her life: time to think.

Introspection is a dangerous drug. Under its influence, Mara left a lucrative studio career that began at Stanford University and the British Film Institute and culminated in supervising the development and production of movies for Warner Bros. and Universal with everyone from Chevy Chase to John Hughes. As she thought about her future and talked with friends who worked in human services, she was struck by the passion they felt for their work and that she lacked for hers. After she got back on her feet, she began mentoring school kids. She felt "more connected" than she ever had before and realized, "I gotta pay attention to this.

"The enlightenment point for me was: One day I was scheduled to go to a meeting, and I realized that I already knew everyone who was going to be there and everything that was going to be said. I knew exactly how everything would turn out, and it seemed like a huge waste of time. Besides, it's a jackpot business—one of the few to put enormous capital at risk with very little research and development—which ends up breeding frenzy and fear at almost every level. The whole town rides upon a sea of fear."

On a Sunday morning in February 1994, Manus drove into downtown Los Angeles to take a tour of Chrysalis, a nonprofit organization that helps economically disadvantaged and homeless individuals become self-supporting through employment opportunities. She began to volunteer there and soon joined the board. While she and her board colleagues were searching for, and interviewing, candidates to run Chrysalis, she came upon a realization that would shock just about everyone who knew and worked with her. It was the job she wanted.

Like many rising stars in the entertainment industry, Manus had been sought after to serve on boards of various nonprofit organizations, but unlike any, she quit her job to actually run one. Now thirty-eight, Manus has been Chrysalis's executive director for four years. "We're there for the people the world is not there for anymore," she explains. Their guiding principle is: A steady job is the single most important step in a homeless person's transition to long-term self-sufficiency. "The main idea behind what we do here," she told the *Los Angeles Times,* "is that it is as important to keep a job as it is to get one. So we offer whatever people need to do that. We provide job leads, but we also offer telephones, typewriters, a computer lab, résumé-writing workshops, and a mail and message center. We give them bus fare and clothes for interviews and teach them how to present themselves in an interview as well as in the workplace."

Though she still wears fashionable business suits and finds time to swim daily to strengthen her back, Manus's change did not come without sacrifice. She sold her house and has never again earned even half as much as she was making when she was twenty-six. With a soft laugh, she describes a once favorite hotel as "the place I used to stay when I made money." But except for the spa vacations that recharged her batteries, she doesn't miss any of it. Money can't buy passion, and there's nothing Manus values more. She lives her life like the character of whom Russian short story writer Isaac Babel wrote: "And Benya Krik had his way, for he was passionate, and passion rules the universe."

"I don't think what I'm doing is necessarily altruistic," Mara told me over spicy rock shrimp at the Border Grill in Santa Monica. We'd met just two weeks earlier at a conference on socially responsive businesses, but I'd followed her work since reading a *People* magazine profile of her earlier that year. "I'm doing it because it makes me crazy that so many people are homeless and poor. I'm doing it because of my own need. I guess selfishly, this makes me feel better."

What is most telling, like the dog that didn't bark in the classic Sherlock Holmes tale, is what Manus did not do. She did not choose to effect change through politics. Her talent, connections, and leadership skills positioned her to be a player in influencing the political process, and it was the established and accepted way of addressing homelessness, poverty, job training, and other social issues. After all, what other options were there? Movie studios have traditionally been breeding grounds for political fund-raisers and young activists. The symbiotic relationship long ago established between Hollywood and politics had been enjoyed by many of Manus's colleagues, but she never considered it an option. Any connection between Congressmen and Senators and the people she cared about most seemed tenuous at best. This may say more about our times than anything that special prosecutors or Larry King could tell us.

Mara Manus's personal journey makes good copy for *People* magazine, but it is only one colorful piece of a broader mosaic just beginning to come into focus and take recognizable form. That mosaic gives us our first picture of a new kind of leadership for the next century that looks very different from anything that has come before. It is servant leadership more than political leadership, community leadership more than national leadership. "Politicians often have conflicting agendas and impose solutions from the top down," Manus says by way of explaining the difference.

"We're listening to the people we serve so that they can play the dominant role in defining their own solutions."

In fact, Manus's experience is almost a perfect fit with the key findings of Peter Hart Research Associates just released in August 1998. On the basis of extensive surveying, the research concluded that "young Americans place a premium on a set of traits that represents an extraordinary break from traditional models of American leadership. . . . Young people see leadership as an exercise available to and, in fact, a responsibility of all Americans, not just a select group of charismatic individuals."

Hart's research, conducted for the youth service organization Public Allies, identified three characteristics of this new approach to leadership. They include:

— an outlook that is distinctly personal, with strong emphasis on direct, one-on-one service, rather than the efforts of their predecessors that focused on broad change of social institutions
— valuing the efficacy of small groups of people working from the bottom up to effect change, and equal participation of all citizens regardless of their authority or position in the community, rather than top-down leadership
— utilizing diversity to formulate solutions

Perhaps most important, according to the survey, "This commitment is not expressed in a vague or amorphous way, but rather it is demonstrated through tangible goals, such as consciously mentoring a young person in the community or actively working with others on a local issue or concern. Nearly seven in ten (68 percent) of young adults report that in the past three years they have been involved in activities to help their community."

Hart's research affirms a fundamentally new vision of leadership for our future. To take root and succeed, it will require new institutions, new communications strategies, and new resources to support it.

Through unconventional personal choices, Manus may have succeeded in casting herself against type. Her actions are admirable, though not necessarily heroic. The impact of one woman and one organization on the structural unemployment wrought by rapid economic change is inherently limited, but together with increasing numbers of others who have chosen similar paths, the future begins to hold the promise of sweeping change.

The past fifteen years have witnessed unprecedented, explosive growth in the number and size of national and community nonprofit organizations. The nonprofit sector now constitutes 10 percent of the American workforce. This was not accidental but rather the result of long-brewing historical forces that culminated in the two presidential terms of Ronald Reagan and the drastic, sweeping reduction of government services that came in the wake of tax cuts and ballooning budget deficits. As always, necessity proved to be the mother of invention. What was invented turned out to be the institutions of a citizen sector whose role was no longer supplementary but central to the resolution of social problems.

American democracy self-corrects, slowly but surely. Scandal sparks reform. The old order, just when it seems most entrenched, invariably yields to the new. Whenever the body politic sprains an ankle, it finds a way to shift its weight to the other one. That is what we're witnessing now in this shift from political activism to direct community service. It is what the history our children read will tell them. It is changing everything from the way our children are being taught in school to how their educations are financed.

Our political institutions are limping badly, but fortunately, a truly vibrant democracy is not made up of political institutions alone. Young people who used to go into politics to change the world are going somewhere else to do it. Where they're going doesn't have a name yet; instead, it has many names. The newer ones alone require their own Yellow Pages to catalog, and in many cases they connote their missions: Empty the Shelters, Food from the 'Hood, Working Today, New Profit Inc., Teach for America, City Year, Citizen Schools, Community Impact!, The Welfare to Work Partnership, SportsBridge, Plugged In, Jumpstart, Free at Last, Do Something, Learning First Alliance, City on a Hill, The Family Van.

Ultimately, new institutions survive and grow only if they are accompanied by new means of supporting them. That's why the future of more than just nonprofits is at stake in creating community wealth. A democracy can only serve all of the people if it provides opportunities for all people to enjoy its abundance. Not everyone is positioned to create personal wealth or be its beneficiary. Not everyone is positioned to create corporate wealth or be its beneficiary. But community wealth reaches into every corner of a community; it is the only tide that truly lifts all boats.

The force of their personalities and the results they've achieved make Mara Manus, Nancy Carstedt, Alan Khazei, Gary Mulhair, Geoffrey Canada, and the others compelling, but to view their roles in a more heroic light would miss the very point. In contrast to an earlier time when they would have been singular exceptions, what they are doing is becoming the rule. Evidence of deep and lasting patterns of change abound. A young man who was part of Teach for America's experiment in building a teacher corps for underserved schools is today managing the effort to save $46 million from the operational side of Philadelphia's public schools. The two men who cofounded City Year's community-service corps in Boston in 1988 have seen it grow to ten cities and become the model for President Clinton's multibillion-dollar AmeriCorps.

Their growing number of contemporaries represent a very different breed from anything that has come before. Unlike their counterparts of the 1960s, they have neither rebelled against the political system nor sought to reform it. More like a parent who finally gives in and does their child's homework, they have sought to cover for it. Even Robert

Kennedy's eldest son, Joe, whose family virtually coined the phrase "to give something back," is leaving Congress to run Citizen's Energy, the nonprofit he founded, and which his brother Michael ran until his death in a skiing accident.

Ashoka founder Bill Drayton argues that social entrepreneurship today is right where the legal profession was before the creation of the bar association. The necessary standards and support systems have yet to be put into place. "The single major evolutionary task that our generation faces," Drayton told *The Atlantic Monthly*, "is developing the democratic revolution's institutions beyond business in the social arena, and people are getting the idea that they can have a career doing that."

These new institutions are responsible for profound change and have become home to thousands of activists committed to rebuilding their neighborhoods and their country, much as political parties once provided a home before being eclipsed by media campaigns on television. These social entrepreneurs are not only finding more effective ways to address social problems; they are redefining democratic participation more profoundly than at any time since Andrew Jackson's populist presidency.

II

The management and leadership expert Peter Drucker estimates that 800,000 new nonprofits have been established over the past thirty years. Bill Drayton is the founder of one such organization: Ashoka, named for the emperor of India who renounced violence and dedicated himself to the public good. Ashoka searches for people whose innovations will lead to large-scale social change and elects them to a fellowship that includes generous financial support as well as professional advice and technical assistance.

Other fellowship programs like those of the MacArthur, Lyndhurst, and Echoing Green foundations make fellowship grants to artists, scientists, and social activists, but none seek to intervene as early and as far upstream in the development of public entrepreneurs as Ashoka, and none get greater leverage for their dollar.

Over seventeen years, Ashoka has elected more than eight hundred fellows from across the world. As Drayton defined them in the preface to a collection of fellow profiles:

> *Leading public/social entrepreneurs are rare men and women who possess the same exceptional levels of vision, creativity, and determination that allow top business entrepreneurs to create entirely or largely new industries. However, they devote these qualities to introducing new solutions to social problems.*
>
> *Traditionally, social organizations have provided charity or relief to the needy or have sought to empower individuals to pursue change neighborhood by neighborhood, farm by farm, or school by school. Feeding the starving and helping the hungry learn how to organize and to grow their own*

food are both essential. But alone they cannot change society's patterns.

Pattern change needs two things: a new idea, and the social entrepreneur who conceives, develops, and champions it over many years. Only through constant, iterative testing and improvement can a good idea become a realistic idea, then a demonstrated success, and finally, after a long marketing effort, the accepted way society works. The faster the world changes, the greater the need for social adaptation— and therefore for social entrepreneurs.

The torch is not just being passed from one generation to another, it is illuminating a new era of citizen service. This is not meant to constitute a premature obituary for American politics, but just the opposite. Obviously, many people, young and old, still participate enthusiastically in the political processes, but for the first time citizen service has emerged as an attractive and effective vehicle for achieving what politics once achieved.

As responsibility for dealing with serious social issues shifts to the grassroots entrepreneurs willing to assume it, don't mistake what they are doing as charity. Traditional charitable organizations like the Salvation Army have always been around to serve the poor. There is nothing new about that. What is new are organizations like Chrysalis that absorb responsibilities once the province of government and go beyond service delivery to create the case for social change. Mara Manus and her colleagues have moved beyond the business of providing charity to building institutions of the future that will create patterns of social change.

Manus is not the first Hollywood studio executive to care about social issues. From superstars like Warren Beatty and Lew Wasserman to prominent political advisers like Marge Tabankin, who once directed the Hollywood Women's Political Committee, there is a long and illustrious tradition of social and political activism at all levels of the entertainment industry, raising money, endorsing candidates, and participating in political campaigns. Wanting to make a difference used to mean participating in some way in the political process. That was then; this is now.

The prohibitive cost of campaign financing, intrusive media scrutiny, and excessive partisan meanness have all but closed off the traditional avenues of democratic participation, leading to detours in their stead. "Unfortunately, all politicians have time to do is campaign for the next election," Manus says, less as an editorial complaint than as a statement of fact. "The process makes such demands on career politicians that the actual work is hard to get around to. . . . No one is engaging people at the bottom of the social structure to participate in defining solutions. We can do that."

Chrysalis concentrates on the poorest of the poor, those it classifies as "living at the very threshold of survival," individuals who have no income at all or receive monthly checks of $212 in general relief for only five months. They are poor candidates to reenter the private workforce. They lack work experience, live in unstable housing situations, and are beset by personal crises such as family breakups, drug abuse, and legal troubles. Before they can get a job they need transitional work experience, stable housing, and intensive case management.

Chrysalis's program is specifically designed to overcome such barriers to employment. It teaches people the most effective ways to obtain work skills that will last a lifetime, using job-hunting classes, instruction in telephone etiquette and grooming, videotaped practice interviews, free use of phones, free bus fare, interview clothes, office supplies, typewriters, and computers. Those who have experienced years of unemployment may need time to develop work ethics and so-called soft skills such as punctuality and the ability to work under supervision. When necessary, Chrysalis offers subsidized employment in maintenance and janitorial programs to reacclimate individuals to the work environment.

So far the results are impressive. Through Chrysalis, twelve hundred formerly homeless individuals have secured employment and returned to productive lives. Seventy-six percent of those participating in their Job Retention Program have maintained employment for eighteen months. Even better, it costs Chrysalis about $1,600 to help one individual gain and maintain employment. By comparison, the state of California's own program costs taxpayers $6,000 per person. Maybe this is why modern management guru Peter Drucker selected Chrysalis to be the case study for his seminar titled "The Nonprofit Leader of the Future." Maybe that's why in September 1998 California

governor Pete Wilson selected Chrysalis for a $1.1 million
grant to move people from welfare to work, citing their
"creative approaches to providing long-term welfare recipients with self-sustaining employment, upward mobility
paths, and higher earning potential."

On a macrolevel, the numbers may not seem very large,
but that is not the point. Manus would never try to convince you that private organizations like Chrysalis should
bear sole responsibility for dealing with all of L.A.'s homeless, but her organization can get close enough to the
people they serve to understand, to innovate, to experiment, and to create the models that do work well enough
to be replicated and perhaps eventually funded, but not
run, by government, so that they can grow to scale.

Still, Manus and her colleagues have no illusions that
what they are doing can replace government. The talent
pool, while growing, is still discouragingly thin. Collaboration is inadequate. Resources are in perpetually short
supply. In Los Angeles County alone, 83,900 children and
adults are homeless on any given night. Chrysalis's downtown office currently turns away over twenty people a
day for lack of space and staffing to serve them. Given
Chrysalis's proven track record in turning lives around,
this is nothing short of tragic. Programs like Chrysalis can
do many things government can't. They can innovate, take
risks, keep close tabs on the people they serve, and let the
experiences of those people shape their methods, but once
their methods are proven to work, only government has
the resources to help them grow. Together, they just might

represent a democracy more finely balanced, steady, and able to serve.

Mara Manus has it all—brains, contacts, energy, and vision. If she'd fallen off her horse in any other decade of the twentieth century, she almost surely would have landed somewhere in politics. Instead, she's inventing institutions of her own, from skid row to Santa Monica, tackling the challenges of inner-city poverty that were once the province of a government that has long since thrown in the towel. Most significant of all, she is not alone.

III

In May 1998, I accompanied Zach's seventh-grade class on a field trip to the new Franklin Roosevelt Memorial. It's never convenient to miss a day of work, but being with your child while he is with friends and classmates is like being in your favorite team's locker room after the game or backstage at a play. You get to hear the way they really talk, to see everything firsthand and unrehearsed, not just what they want you to see.

My taxi dropped me at the Roosevelt Memorial, alongside the Potomac River, about twenty minutes before the arrival of the entire seventh grade. (I passed on riding the school bus—there are some things even an interested parent doesn't want to see.) Getting there early gave me a chance to look at the memorial's fountains and massive granite walls engraved with quotations from FDR's four terms. The memorial is divided into four corresponding outdoor galleries, or rooms, with walls of red South Dakota granite. Huge blocks of stone are piled in places along the seven-acre path as if to suggest the Herculean nature of what Roosevelt built, from the post-Depression economic recovery to victory in World War II.

One of the passages, over a sculpture of a Great Depression breadline, was familiar: "The test of our progress is not whether we add more to the abundance of those who have much, it is whether we provide enough to those who have too little." Because of the Depression, Roosevelt probably did more to address hunger in America than any other president. The twin threats of total economic collapse and Nazi aggression made the present perilous and the future fragile in the 1930s and 1940s. Older Americans who lived through and remember those times find this memorial powerful and moving. I wondered if it would mean anything at all to Zach and his friends.

When the buses pulled up with about one hundred seventh graders, Zach's teacher handed me a chaperon's manual and a list of the seven children in my group: Tiffany, Scott, Matt, Lauren, Cherell, Joey, and, of course, Zach. Until that moment, it simply hadn't occurred to me that I'd have responsibility for other students as well. The challenge of supervising Zach is generally so all-consuming that it doesn't permit such luxuries. Nevertheless, I wanted to be helpful, so I quickly switched my strategy from man-to-man to zone defense.

Several days of careful thought had gone into which kids would be grouped together. The groups were strategically balanced to account for friendships, animosities, gender, and Ritalin use. Seven kids is a lot to oversee, but I could tell right away that the girls would be easy. They huddled together closely, talked softly, and moved as a unit, as if choreographed. Girls at this age are like a solar system, with one bright, shining leader in the center around which everyone else revolves in a gravitational orbit. Boys, on the other hand, are more like the Big Bang, exploding out in all directions and moving farther away with each passing moment. With my list in hand, I shouted after the boys to establish who was who. Joey looked at me and with a poker face said he was Matt. Matt needed no other cue to claim he was Joey. The tone of the trip was set for the rest of the day.

Zach's class must have thought Franklin Roosevelt was the thirty-second playground builder of the United States, instead of the thirty-second president. Fresh off the bus, with a day's stored energy released by sunshine, they ran and pushed and raced ahead to climb rocks, pull themselves onto ledges, balance on the edge of fountains, be the first to the next area. I made a couple of casual stabs at explaining the significance of a statue or quotation, but they were past even pretending to be interested. Zach was born the same number of years from Franklin Roosevelt's inauguration as my father was from Lincoln's! This was ancient history to them.

Doubtless there are many things that would surprise Roosevelt were he alive today. Poverty wouldn't necessarily be one of them. His presidency was engulfed and defined by it, but poverty in the midst of unprecedented prosperity would surely leave him perplexed. Days after Zach's field trip, *The New York Times* published a major front-page story headlined AS ECONOMY BOOMS, MIGRANT WORKERS' HOUSING WORSENS. It described how Immokalee, Florida, draws thousands of migrant workers each winter for the tomato and pepper harvest. SOS funds a shelter in Immokalee, which I visited early this year. The *Times* story included color pictures showing the insides of trailers I saw on my visit, where migrant workers live ten to a room and hang their food from strings nailed to the ceiling to keep it from rats.

It is estimated that about 800,000 of the 2.5 million farmworkers in the United States lack adequate shelter. The *Times* explained that the workforce has changed in ways that make it difficult for the government to improve living conditions. Once mostly American, it is now largely made up of immigrants from Mexico and Central America, 40 percent of them here illegally. They put up with the living conditions for the opportunity to earn ten times what they could at home. "The economic imperative driving them—that they can lift their families out of poverty—is so powerful that it has assured a plentiful supply of migrants even as real farm wages have fallen," according to the *Times*. "The root of the problem is there is an oversupply of farm workers," said Bruce Goldstein of the Farmworkers Justice Fund in Washington.

Having walked the dirt roads and trailer camps of

Immokalee, I can tell you that the squalid conditions are not much different from what history tells us Roosevelt once faced and sought to address. What is different today is the lack of political will to do something about it, and the failure of our political leadership to even attempt to marshal such will. In the midst of an expanding economy that is the envy of the world, our moral stature is shrinking. Ancient history or not, more than just America's school-children need to absorb why Roosevelt's greatness has been memorialized and honored today. Seventh graders can't be expected to pay attention to what both the president and Congress ignore.

On the way back to the bus, I could find only six of the charges in my care. Zach had dropped back and was standing near a bench with a girl named Sophie. It looked like he was holding her hand, but I assumed I'd just been out in the sun too long. I went to the bus and waited for him to board. I looked at my watch. The field trip was young. There were still five hours to go.

A few months later, I woke up early on Labor Day morning. The morning was cool, and the streets of the neighborhood were especially quiet. At 7:00 A.M., the Sunday *New York Times* lay stuffed in its blue wrapper at the bottom of the driveway. It was thicker than I expected. Holiday weekends are usually heavy on picnics and light on news, but that day, there was coverage of the Swissair plane crash in Nova Scotia, terrorism, Russia's economic collapse,

Mark McGwire's home-run race, and, of course, the Monica Lewinsky scandal.

Ken Starr's report was soon to be delivered to congressional authorities. The columnists were rejuvenated, speculating as they had for a month of Sundays that the scandal engulfing the Clinton administration was reaching its climactic and conclusive stage.

Senators, political consultants, unnamed White House staff, and editorial writers all had advice for the president, the special prosecutor, and each other So did historians, business leaders, ministers, and college professors. There were confident, seemingly certain opinions regarding what authority the president retained, the credibility of our foreign policy, and the role of the media. A few new careers were launched on CNN, just as they were during the O. J. Simpson trial. Book contracts were being negotiated and announced.

Everyone had a course of action to recommend as the best course for the country. "The president should apologize." "Congress should censure or rebuke." "Starr's report should include an executive summary." Conveniently for those doing the recommending, the course of action being advocated was always a course of action to be taken by someone else. The opinions were diverse, wide-ranging, and often diametrically opposed. Some were sober and wise, others shrill and strident, but they all had one thing in common: They were aimed away. The focus was external. The finger pointed to others. No one had looked inward and felt moved or compelled to speak out about what they would now do differently to make America better, stronger, or sounder. Yet each of us has the capacity to do just that.

The beauty of a democracy like ours is that everyone is free to have an opinion about what should be done in the national interest. What's as beautiful, though perhaps less apparent, is that everyone is free to do more than have an opinion. Everyone is also free to actually serve the national interest by serving their community.

Increasingly, a new generation of Americans are not only expressing their opinions, but also their citizenship, by personally embracing service. Whether through Habitat for Humanity, Teach for America, or a thousand other vehicles, there is building, healing, tutoring, teaching, and training taking place on a scale unprecedented in our history. It is not an adequate substitute for government. Volunteers at a maternal and child health clinic cannot take the place of comprehensive health-care legislation that a strong president and cooperative Congress could enact. But they can make a difference to the underweight child they diagnose or the parent seeking referral to other available services.

What if everyone who had an opinion about Bill Clinton also had a firm idea about what they themselves could do to make America better, whether it was mentoring an at-risk student, volunteering at a homeless shelter, or reading to a child? What if they discussed their own service to community with the same intensity because they understood that, in the long run, it might be every bit as consequential? It would be too remarkable a shock to hear Sam Donaldson, Senate majority leader Trent Lott, or any of the talking heads respond in such fashion to breaking political developments. In fact, it is so unimaginable as to sound naive if not ludicrous. What is more remarkable is that thousands of ordinary Americans have responded precisely that way—not in response to Clinton, but in reaction to nearly three decades of a political system deteriorating from special-interest money and mean-spirited partisanship. They've rolled up their sleeves and plunged into new neighborhoods to work with people of different colors, different educations and incomes, and different life experiences.

Washington is a city where more history is made and less is remembered than anywhere on the planet. If there is anything to be learned from the flawed or failed presidencies of the last four decades, it's that there is too much at stake in our democracy to relegate its fate to only one man's hands. The Founding Fathers considered this core theory. In their day, it was easier to implement. The media now make the president such a pervasive part of our daily life that the connection between his welfare and ours seems impossible to overstate. In fact, a healthy civil society offers a more balanced dynamic.

In his speech to the National Press Club three years ago, former New Jersey senator Bill Bradley warned "of the temptation offered by the 'knight in shining armor.' . . . He or she might make us feel better momentarily, but then if we are only spectators thrilled by the performance how have we progressed collectively? A character in Bertolt

Brecht's *Galileo* says, 'Pity the nation that has no heroes,' to which Galileo responds, 'Pity the nation that needs them.' All of us have to go out in the public square, and all of us have to assume our citizenship responsibilities."

Labor Day is one of our most unusual holidays. It does not celebrate the achievements of a great and famous leader like Washington, Lincoln, or King. It does not recall the heroism of Memorial Day or Veterans Day. Rather, Labor Day honors the ordinary, day-in-and-day-out, otherwise uncelebrated work of millions of anonymous men and women whose individual acts and ethics are understood to make our country great. They are the engine of our economy. They are the engine of our democracy, too. Any one of us can change America by our actions.

Those who dismiss the impact that a single individual can have would have be sobered by the remembrance of one of the Swissair plane crash victims, Jonathan Mann, the pioneering international advocate who is credited with almost single-handedly instigating the global mobilization against AIDS. A colleague of Mann's, quoted in the *New York Times* obituary, remembered one of his most characteristic remarks: "People say there is no use trying to change the world. But if we don't try, will it change?"

What matters is not whether fewer talk and more serve. What matters is how each of us sees our place in a maturing democracy. A strong America needs good government and a better president. We should never stop working for both, but we need to be better citizens too. The country waited for Ken Starr's report, so that our leaders could get back on course. But AIDS isn't waiting, hunger isn't waiting, illiteracy isn't waiting, and most of us need not wait either.

The danger of expecting heroics from our leaders, besides their obvious human fallibility, is that we expect less from ourselves. I'm as interested as anybody else in what Senator Joe Lieberman thinks the president ought to say, or what CNN's Greta Van Sustern thinks the appellate court should do, but when it comes time to figure out how to get the country back on track, what if instead of staring into the television, we stared into the mirror?

When my daughter, Mollie, was six years old, she would help me walk our dogs around our neighborhood. The suburban subdivision in which we live is like one large cul-de-sac of nearly three hundred homes, and it takes about twenty minutes to complete the loop.

Mollie helped by walking about ten paces behind me, swinging her arms and legs, and twittering nonstop about her gym teacher, cold pizza at lunch, the stars, the boy who kicks her desk, and the injustice of not owning her own horse before she turned seven. Her jacket would hang open. She was too young to be cold.

We have two large Great Pyrenees that together tip the vet's scale at 265 pounds. They are gentle dogs but strong, and their leashes must be held by me. They sleep no more than twenty-four hours a day, but are always up for a walk. They seem to figure out that we are going to go for a walk at the same time I do, if not just a moment before, exquisitely sensitive to such nuances as me tying my shoes or reaching for the house key.

One cold night in January, under a beautiful full moon, we began at our usual pace, me struggling to keep the dogs off our neighbors' lawns, Mollie behind me working to keep up and to keep her train of thought from jumping tracks.

"Look at that moon, Dad," she said from behind me. "Do you think that Grandpa Nate is up there?"

My father had died just a few weeks before, and although we hadn't discussed it much since, I had a general idea of where she was headed.

"I don't know, Molls. Why do you ask?"

"Well, I think he's up there. That's where the angels are," she explained, "and so I think Grandpa Nate is up there with them. Do you, Dad?"

"Oh, I don't know, honey. I guess it would be nice to think so. Nothing wrong with that."

We continued to walk, zigging and zagging but keeping the same space between us, Mollie speaking loudly enough that I could hear her without turning around.

"Oh, Dad," she said with a new strain of excitement in her voice. "Did you know that Grandpa Nate was in Martin Luther King's band?"

For the first time that evening, I'd been stopped in my tracks. I turned to look at her but she did not yet make eye contact.

"What did you say, Molls?"

"I said did you know that Grandpa Nate was in Martin Luther King's band?"

"Martin Luther King's band?" Now we had both stopped.

"Yeah."

"You mean, like, he played an instrument?" I asked incredulously.

"Yeah, I guess so."

"What instrument?"

"I don't know," she said dismissively, as if it wasn't important.

I decided that by the time we got around the cul-de-sac and got back home I would try to figure out what in the world she was talking about. A child's stream of consciousness can leave a trail as clear as a raccoon's from the trash can if you pay close enough attention to it.

It was January, and days earlier the country had celebrated Martin Luther King's birthday as a national holiday. This had to be relevant. I asked Mollie if her mom had discussed Dr. King at all, perhaps one morning while they were driving to school.

"Yeah."

It would have been like her to find some connection for the kids. I only had one theory and I took a crack at it.

"Did Mom tell you that Grandpa Nate went to Martin Luther King's march on Washington?" The night before King gave his "I Have a Dream" speech at the Lincoln Memorial was the only night of my childhood that my dad did not spend in his own bed. His trip, with a delegation of Pittsburghers, and everything he told us about it when he came home has been an essential part of our family history ever since.

"Uh-huh."

And then it hit me. To a six-year-old, being in a "march" and being in a band are just about synonymous. Grandpa Nate had not been in Martin Luther King's band after all. I explained the difference to Mollie. I've always been glad I caught it when I did. She might have gone to college thinking my dad played trombone with Martin Luther King and the All-Stars. When we got back to the house, I asked Mollie what she knew about Martin Luther King anyway.

"Not so so much, Dad," which was the way she talked then.

"Well, anything at all?" I pressed.

"I know that he was a hero," she said, not looking up from the toy she was playing with at the kitchen table. "He was a hero because he helped people."

That was good enough for me. She was just six years old. For now, she didn't need to know much more than that. I was content to let it sit there, but she wasn't.

"Dad?"

"Hmmm?"

"Who are the heroes today?"

Now I'd been stopped in my tracks twice. Who *are* the heroes today? You've read about some of them in this book. They are not the same as the rich and the famous. But that's not what Mollie asked. They are not the same as celebrities. But Mollie didn't ask that either. Most important of all, though many are singled out here, they are not singular, even though they are exceptional.

CHAPTER TEN

When a Rock Pile
Ceases to Be a Rock Pile

I

I've come to Washington National Cathedral to finish writing my book. I park the Jeep on Massachusetts Avenue, and as I cross the street and walk up the sidewalk, the cathedral looms too large to take in. Built upon the highest ground in Washington, its massive walls and towers capture all of the morning light. Designed and built in the same style and manner as medieval churches, stone on stone with no structural steel, the 514-foot-long cathedral is the sixth largest in the world. Behind its twin bell towers flow football fields of limestone, marble, and brick. It took more than eighty years to get it all here.

L'Enfant's plan for the capital city, commissioned by President George Washington, envisioned a national church, but it wasn't until 1905 that the site was purchased, and, in 1907, the foundation stone laid. For the next eighty years, railroad cars and trucks brought limestone from a quarry in Bloomington, Indiana, chosen for its even grade and adaptability to hand-carving.

With the possible exception of the Lincoln Memorial, which is diminutive by comparison, this is the one spot in Washington—much of which was built on reclaimed swampland—that feels solid, anchored. It is a fifty-seven-acre oasis of permanence in a town where transience is the norm, where even the most powerful come, but also, inevitably, go. The commerce and culture of Washington are organized around the rhythm of arrival and departure, but this cathedral is not going anywhere. The sixty-three carillon and English bells alone weigh two hundred tons. This cathedral has weight and strength. It is dependable, immovable.

The cathedral opens to the public at 10:00 A.M., and at 10:01 I am passing through the central portal whose round arch above the tympanum is graced by sculptor Frederick Hart's relief carving of the creation of man. The half-formed figures of men and women, handsome and sensuous, determined in their struggle, are swirling in a cloudy maelstrom of creative force whose turmoil ebbs only once you pass under it. I'm amazed at how lifelike the sculpture is, how smooth and soft the flesh of these stone figures are. The lines in the hands and forearms, the curves of breast and hip, suggest a master carver's greatest work.

I take a seat in the second pew past the transept and sit with a small leather-bound journal in my lap. High above, at every intersection of ribs in the vaulting is an elaborately carved circular stone called a boss. I find one that measures five feet across showing Moses holding the Ten Commandments. The sun streams in from the east through stained-glass windows. They are almost too bright to stare at, vivid primary colors, at times seemingly bursting into flame, changing moment by moment as the positions of sun, clouds, and earth change.

The cathedral is already filling with tourists. A woman from India sits across the aisle from me wearing her traditional sari and talking on a cell phone. A young mother with a backpack follows her baby, who scampers and bends to touch the floor's colorful pieces of marble, which have come from quarries in Vermont, Tennessee, Maryland, and Italy. People are talking, but voices cannot really be heard. Instead, the walls echo as if the visitors were walking across God's drum. It's easy to imagine how, in the Middle Ages, cathedrals of such size became the crossroads of an emerging urban civilization. It is where hospitals, social service agencies, and universities all originated.

The stained-glass windows are stunning. There are more than two hundred of them. They reflect not just the history of one faith, or even all faiths, but rather the faith in what's learned from history. The panels depict Moses as well as Jesus, the Torah as well as the New Testament. The Civil War is depicted and so is the United Nations. One glass panel even has a piece of moon rock embedded in it. Woodrow Wilson is buried here, as is Helen Keller. Lincoln is commemorated, as is Martin Luther King. The cathedral seems to be a monument to all who struggled to set the spirit free.

The beauty of the cathedral belies the struggle required to complete it. The stock market crash of 1929, America's entry into World War II, the eventual deaths of the original architects, and persistent shortages of funding all interrupted and delayed construction. In a controversial decision grounded less in faith than in his savvy insight into human nature, the dean of the cathedral, Francis Sayre, Jr., decided to devote the limited funding available in the 1960s to completing the central tower instead of the nave, which is the main body of the church where the congregation sits. In a way, it would mean building the cathedral backward. But Dean Sayre was a rule-breaker, an entrepreneur. It was his conviction that "the tower would build the nave," that its dominating presence in the sky would serve to inspire the donors to come forward with the remaining necessary funding. Indeed, when the tower was dedicated in 1964, contributions steadily increased.

I've come back to Washington National Cathedral for the same reason I studied the cathedral in Milan a year ago, and for the same reason Santa Monica, Chicago, Boston, Seattle, Denver, and Harlem have been part of my itinerary. After two decades devoted to public service, the desire is not just to serve, but to make that service count. I've wanted to understand the strategies and secrets of those whose efforts endure, who have built lasting, sustainable institutions to nourish both community and soul, whose cathedrals still stand. And I've wanted to share that understanding with anyone who is working to make their community, their country, and themselves better.

There is no formula for building cathedrals. No two are alike, nor would we want them to be. And so, a formula is not what I offer here, but I'm not offering just a metaphor, either. There are lessons to be learned from the essential principles that guided the cathedral builders and enabled their work to not only inspire but endure. Many of those lessons are being carried forward today by people like Nancy Carstedt, Alan Khazei, Geoffrey Canada, and others who have been included in these pages. They are specific, concrete lessons that we can test and measure whether we are applying them or not.

First, cathedral building is a lifetime commitment, but it's not only the cathedral builders who need to understand that. Those who support cathedral builders, from large foundations to individual donors, must reorient their support and funding strategies toward long-term, reliable, and sustained support that remains available until an agreed-upon outcome is achieved, rather than the three-to-five-year cycles of grant-making that are most typical today. To earn the confidence of their supporters, cathedral builders need to work back from a larger vision of what they are trying to accomplish; they must share Dean Sayre's conviction that "the tower would build the nave," and convey a strategic vision of the outcomes they conceive. Short-term efforts do not create lasting change. Like the cathedral builders, masons, and stone carvers, our most important work may take our entire lifetime, and even then we may not see the final results of our efforts. There are many ways I know that to be true, but more so as a parent than any other. There's no work I can do that is more important than the joyful work of being Zach and Mollie's dad. It is day-in, day-out work, and I will be long gone before either is "finished." But that doesn't detract from my dedication to my vision for them. Indeed, it enhances it.

Second, the most successful efforts to create social change are more rather than less inclusive, drawing on the shared strength of not just the experts but the entire community. Like Alan Khazei at City Year, Noel Cunningham in Denver, and the staff and board of Share Our Strength, cathedral builders see strengths to share in rich and poor, black and white, skilled and unskilled, and they design and create vehicles for them to do so.

Third, most of the world's cathedrals, including Washington National Cathedral, are literally built upon the foundations laid by others. The small St. Albans church stood where the National Cathedral stands today. The cathedral of Santa Maria Maggiore stood where the great duomo stands in Milan today. Cathedral builders do not start from scratch and do not reinvent the wheel. The most successful nonprofits, those that are built to last, incorporate the research, techniques, and methods of others that came before in conscious and deliberate ways. They look to collaborate and add to what has already been built.

Fourth, cathedral builders sustain their work by creating their own wealth. Like Gary Mulhair at Pioneer Human Services, they do not rely solely on donations, handouts, or redistributed wealth, but instead generate new community wealth.

Fifth, like Geoffrey Canada, Marian Wright Edelman, Dr. Martin Luther King, and others, cathedral builders commit themselves to telling stories that convey values and best practices to those who come after them.

Finally, the great cathedrals incorporate all of these. As social scientist Lisbeth Schorr writes in *Common Purpose,* "The time has come to give up searching for a single intervention that will be the one-time fix—the lifetime inoculation—that will protect against the effects of growing up in neighborhoods of despair, violence, and unemployment, in neighborhoods without decent schools, safe streets, stable families, or a sense of community. Forget about selecting among economic development, public safety, physical rehabilitation, community building, education reform, or service reform in an effort to find the single most promising way to intervene. . . . Take a broader view."

II

Antoine de Saint-Exupéry once said, "A rock pile ceases to be a rock pile the moment a single man contemplates it, bearing within him the image of a cathedral." As I exit Washington National Cathedral through the same door I entered, I walk past the stone carvers' cottage, across the sidewalk from the cathedral's western portal. It is a small, white, one-room cottage that looks as if it belongs at the beach. Large blocks of stone can be seen tumbled beside and behind it. There is one man working inside, chiseling away at a statuette that will soon become part of the cathedral. The statuette is maybe two feet tall, and the plaster model he works from is on a table next to it. He is bent over, using the chisel to bring out a subtle line of a shoe. His concentration is intense. He is master carver Vincent Palumbo, and I am astonished to have the chance to watch him work. His father was a cathedral carver, and he has trained dozens of young apprentices in the stone-carving skills necessary to complete the thousands of carvings that decorate the cathedral.

The room he is in—white floor and ceiling and white walls—is almost empty, except for four small wooden platforms on which he carves. Wearing blue jeans and a green checked shirt, he has a thick mustache and sideburns that have either gone gray or are flecked with limestone dust. On the shelf behind him I count about 180 different chisels and blades, a few brushes, and other tools. They all look the same to me, but after watching him work and repeatedly choose one over the other, I see the appreciation for nuance that earned him his title of master. On the wall behind him sits a shelf near the ceiling. Champagne bottles in a long row bear the names of stone carvers who celebrated each New Year's Eve from 1961 until the cathedral's completion in 1990.

All the time I've been standing there, just inches away

on the other side of a thin pane of glass, his concentration has been intense. He looks up once and our eyes meet, but it is not even an instant. This may be Vincent Palumbo's ten-thousandth carving, a statuette to be placed high and almost out of sight, but he must get it exactly right. As his predecessor, Roger Morigi, once explained: "A stone carver is inclined to be an honest man. An executive may embellish his résumé, but a stone carver's work is there for all to see. No matter how well he writes, it does not change the quality of his carving."

It has been hours since I parked the Jeep across the street, and though I've finished the writing I came to do, I don't know how to leave. After months of visits, I've just begun to know this place. So much of it has been revealed, but there is so much more the National Cathedral promises to tell me. It is too much to understand in one day or one hundred. I get the eerie sense that, if nothing else, this is what the cathedral wants me to know. But that's not all this cathedral has taught me. Though situated at Washington's highest elevation, it is easily accessible to all. Though it took fortune on top of fortune to build, it can be enjoyed for free. And though its glory may be shared by all, the joy and peace it yields more than fills all the available space within.

The task at hand looks to be a relatively minor one for Vincent Palumbo, certainly in comparison to supervising the carving of Frederick Hart's magnificent tympanum, which I later learned was also Palumbo's work. But he is not treating it as minor. Although the cathedral was deemed officially finished when the last stone was set twenty-six stories above the ground on September 29, 1990, Palumbo's work is not finished. Never mind that the construction crews have been disbanded. Never mind that the attention and accolades bestowed by President Bush and others are now almost a decade old. Vincent Palumbo chips and chisels away, one small piece of limestone at a time. The cathedral just outside his window may be finished, but not the cathedral within.

Afterword

About three weeks before the hardcover edition of *The Cathedral Within* arrived in bookstores, my editor sent me two bound copies from the first print run, along with a complimentary note. I knew just what I would do with the books. On the blank pages just inside their front covers, I wrote separate—and predictably sentimental—letters to both my children. As the book includes stories about each of them, I said, "It's great to have children you want to tell the world about." At ages fourteen and ten, Zach and Mollie were too young to be expected to read the book. But I thought my short letter would suffice for the moment, and I hoped they'd come to appreciate the book itself at a later time.

"Thanks, Pop," Zach said as he took the book from me without looking at it and tossed it across the room, all in one smooth motion, the way you release a Frisbee just as soon as you grasp it. The brand-new book landed in a pile of debris consisting of dirty clothes, hockey pads and pucks, other discarded books, and magazines. It blended in so perfectly that I feared it might not be noticed for weeks. (Mollie, with her characteristically greater sense of decorum, placed her unopened book on a crowded book-shelf, where it achieved equal invisibility.)

"Ahem." I cleared my throat. "Oh, I, uh, wrote a little note in it for you, buddy," I said casually, not wanting to make more of it than it was.

"Sure, I'll read it later, Pops." As with most kids, "later" was Zach's favorite time zone, a kind of Promised Land for homework, changing clothes, or shoveling snow, a point somewhere out on the horizon that seemed to recede with each step toward it. The next day, when I walked into his room, I noticed that the book lay undisturbed, precisely where it had touched down from its brief flight. That evening, while tucking Zach in, I couldn't resist a glance out of the corner of my eye. The book had not been moved by so much as a fraction of an inch.

And there it sat, day after day, like an abandoned car on the wrong side of town that might go forever unclaimed. My obsession grew; I even considered laying a matchstick or thread across it, like movie detectives who want to know whether a door has been opened.

Then again, in many ways writing a book like *The Cathedral Within* is like knocking on many doors at once and waiting to see which of them opens. I've spent the last two years walking through some of those doors that did in fact open. What I learned from the reaction to the book became as interesting to me as anything I had tried to share in writing it. These lessons are too varied and extensive to all be included here, but this book would no longer feel complete without the inclusion of at least a few examples.

I expected the audience for the book to be social

workers, teachers, anti-poverty advocates, and others who work in the nonprofit sector—and I do know from their e-mails, letters, and speaking invitations that this book resonated with them. But the majority of people I heard from were doctors, lawyers, Wall Street bankers, and other professionals who were looking to make a change in their lives. More Americans than I could have imagined are seeking ways to share their strength and build their cathedrals, for ways to transform their lives by giving something back.

One e-mail I received—both typical of the responses and extraordinary at the same time—was from a man named Everett Spees. "In reading through *The Cathedral Within* I was very struck by the parallels to my own experience in finding ways to give something back. . . . Briefly, I am a retired transplant surgeon (since January 1998). I was previously chief of organ transplants at Walter Reed U.S. Army Medical Center, and subsequently held professorships at Johns Hopkins and the University of Colorado Health Sciences Center. I was in surgery for 42 years. Four years ago, I was ordained as a priest, a lifelong dream of mine."

Dr. Spees went on to explain that while undergoing chaplain training, he had been assigned to a nonprofit children's psychiatric hospital in Colorado. "These children have experienced so much neglect, abuse, and deprivation that many have never been told a story or been given any instruction by adult role models in negotiation or considering the morality or consequences of the decisions they make. They are prematurely sexualized and often brutalized, and have lost their schools, their religious associations, their families, and their innocence." In describing his new work with the kids at the clinic, many of whom were so damaged they'd attempted suicide, he wrote: "This work has been transforming for me. I enjoy it as much as transplanting organs."

He concluded by offering, "If you had a chance to visit, I believe you would be surprised at the wonderful things that are happening for children who are greatly distressed and damaged."

I couldn't resist.

Dr. Spees has the steady, deliberate demeanor of the surgeon he was for nearly half a century. He planned our day like an operation, leaving little to chance, ensuring we'd see what we needed to see for an accurate diagnosis. We talked to the hospital's administrators and educators and toured the campus, classrooms, and residential units. Almost every wall in the place was covered with handwritten reminders of rules, procedures, times to do things, and "self-control sequences." Structure was a valued commodity, and the "quiet rooms" in each and every building, whose doors swung open to reveal barren views, provided a substitute for structure when all else failed. The patients, in jeans and T-shirts, looked like kids anywhere, though most were on meds—there was little sign of the aggression, violence, or self-destructive tendencies that had landed them here.

Fourteen states send their most troubled kids to this clinic. Most of these children are between the ages of seven and fourteen, and they have been in "the system" their entire lives. For many, it is this or jail. Fifteen years ago the average length of stay, which doctors complained was too short, was seventy-six days. Today it is about fifteen to twenty days; for many, it is just five. The insurance constraints of managed care push many kids out the door before they're ready. Too often a discharge is predicated on essential outpatient services that in fact are nonexistent.

"These are the people that will be the homeless population ten years from now," an administrator said with certainty. Many of the "kiddos," as the staff affectionately called them, will struggle with mental-health issues their whole lives. During a drawn-out explanation of the continuum of care, budgets, and changes in insurance, and of the kinds of services the hospital wished it could provide but doesn't, Dr. Spees interrupted for the first and only time of the day to punctuate the point. "This is about saving children's lives," he said quietly.

I asked Dr. Spees if he missed surgery. "No, forty-two years was enough," he said without a moment's hesitation. "You never get to sleep, because you're jumping on planes at all hours to harvest organs." Then he explained his own connection to this psychiatric clinic. In the course of harvesting organs for transplant, he came to realize that one of the largest categories of donors was adolescent suicides. It shocked and sickened him to be taking these organs.

Colorado has the third highest adolescent suicide rate in the country. Nobody seems to have even a theory, let alone an adequate explanation, as to why. Dr. Spees tried to convey how little hope the kids have, and how far we are from even being able to understand or relate to such despair: "I do a values group, tell stories, and try to get the kids to talk about their lives. Afterwards I ask the kids to tell me what their happiest memories were, and what were their worst memories. One twelve-year-old boy said: 'My happiest memories are the ones I can't remember. My worst are all the rest.'

"I have become ever more aware of the financial precariousness of this nonprofit institution that cares for three hundred children," Spees told me. "If there was a way for this institution to create community wealth, we might be able to develop programs and keep the staff we need to succeed. . . . If this hospital closed, the repercussions in the community would be devastating. More and more children would be shut up in jails, and many children would be dead of suicide, homicide, gangs, and drug deals; and many of the girls would go the next small step to prostitution and life in crack houses."

Spees's exasperation hung in the air like a punt at Denver's Mile High Stadium. He's devoted more than four decades to salvaging life where others saw only carnage. His hands have literally reached deep into other human beings to search for hope and strength that can be shared. Through his entire career, his surgical skills have enabled him to fix things. A sick child could be made well by taking out a faulty organ and stitching in a good one. Not as simple as changing a car battery, but the impact was almost as immediate. Cause and effect were clearly understood. Long hours, dedicated staff, and well-rehearsed procedures predicted a certain result. But it doesn't work that way in a psychiatric hospital. We can't yet do for the soul what we do for the liver. This takes longer. It's more expensive. Some cathedrals are never finished.

On the November morning in 2000 that a Florida judge, Terry Lewis, ruled in favor of certifying George W. Bush's election, I was in a hotel ballroom in Washington, D.C., giving a keynote speech to the Society of American Foresters. That's right, foresters. Seventeen hundred of them.

It had felt like a stretch when, at the urging of an enthusiastic neighbor who serves as their communications director and who had read *The Cathedral Within,* I was invited to speak. This was the foresters' hundredth annual conference, and they were inaugurating a policy of sending their members out for an afternoon of service after the morning's meetings. They would be giving talks in schools, building Habitat for Humanity houses, and maintaining nature trails. They hoped I'd provide a rousing sendoff.

As I walked into the ballroom, I could hear one of the early arrivals snap his index finger against the program. He shook his head, turned to the man next to him, and said, "Guess now we got something about using this stuff to build cathedrals." I described to the attendees, who were older than the audiences I'm accustomed to, the cathedral-building concept. I mentioned the old Greek proverb that says, "A society grows great when men plant trees whose shade they know they shall never sit in." That's about as close to cathedral building as you can get with foresters. I made it through forty-five minutes, and so did they.

As usual, what was interesting was not what I had to say but what *they* had to say. Afterward, as I was signing books, an older man, with bright white hair and mustache, told me that his son was resisting the pressure of friends and family to make more money, because he was devoted to the rehabilitation work he was doing with prisoners. The man asked if I could inscribe the book in a specific way. "I'm not trying to put words in your mouth, but something that affirms he's made the right choice would sure be the encouragement he needs to hear right now."

The supervisor of a National Forest in Utah asked for ideas on how to create service opportunities for kids. An agricultural student from Stevens Point, Wisconsin, said she wanted to find a place to volunteer. A woman who planted seedlings for Weyerhaeuser wondered if there were ways to get her company involved in a community project. A young man who told me he was legally blind asked if I could get him a recording of *The Cathedral Within*.

Ninety minutes later, I was still standing there fielding questions. Nobody else seemed to share my obsession with the Florida court's ruling. While millions of Americans waited to learn who would lead them, I was with a room full of Americans eager to learn how they could lead.

There has been a lot of commentary about how the narrow margin in the 2000 presidential election finally demonstrated that every individual vote makes a difference for the future of our country. That is true, and a very powerful idea. But voting is just one act and responsibility of citizenship. The larger lesson is that not just every vote, but every act of citizenship, makes a difference and could determine the future. Service is an act of citizenship. Philanthropy is an act of citizenship. Volunteering is an act of citizenship. Communicating your views to your representatives in the House and Senate is an act of citizenship. And just like a single vote or a handful of votes, one act or a handful of such acts can ultimately change the world. As in the case of the ballots cast in Florida, none of us have the luxury of knowing in advance when and where a certain action, whether a vote or an act of service, will be the lever that shifts the planet, but the laws of physics are immutable: Put force against a lever, and something moves.

One day much closer to his sixteenth birthday, Zach brushed by me in the kitchen and, without ever stopping or even looking at me, said, "Hey, Pops . . . read four chapters . . . not bad."

"Four chapters of what?" I asked, thinking that maybe he'd finally cracked the tenth-grade Ancient Civilization textbook upon which he would soon be tested.

"Your book."

"Which one?" I wondered, assuming now that he'd found a novel in my study or the backseat of my car.

"*Your* book. *The Cathedral Within.* Yeah, I saw J.D. reading it at school and thought I should take a look."

At the school Zach attends, a group of parents interested in devising community wealth strategies to offset tuition increases had been circulating the book. Obviously, J.D.'s parents had passed the book along to their son, a classmate of Zach's. It had been nearly two years since that first hot-off-the-press copy I'd given Zach had found its almost permanent resting place in a cluttered corner of his room.

Zach is not all that has changed and grown.

Many of the organizations described in this book—Share Our Strength, City Year, Chrysalis, the Chicago Children's Choir, Pioneer Human Services, the Rheedlen Centers, and others—not only have expanded significantly but have begun to wisely and courageously invest in themselves and in their own capacity so that they will become self-sustainable and better able to serve more of those in need. Community Wealth Ventures, for instance, has made the transition from being an experimental consulting practice to being an experienced and successful firm with a dozen staff members and a waiting list of clients determined to leverage their assets in ways that create new wealth for themselves and their communities.

Despite fluctuations in the stock market, significant wealth created from the new economy has doubled the assets of charitable foundations and led to the creation of thousands of new philanthropic efforts, including in the new field of venture philanthropy, which applies venture-capital practices and strategic management assistance to help effective nonprofit organizations get to scale.

For many people, it is only after they finally attain material wealth that they realize that material wealth by itself is not enough to fulfill them. As Cesar Chavez said on the morning in 1968 when he broke his fast for justice for the farm workers who grow and harvest our food: "When we are really honest with ourselves we must admit that our lives are all that really belong to us, so it is how we use our lives that determines what kind of men we are. It is my deepest belief that only by giving our lives do we find life."

Resource Directory

I. There are many wonderful organizations in communities across the country that exemplify the principles of cathedral building. A sampling includes:

American Red Cross
430 17th Street NW
Washington, DC 20006
703-206-6000
www.redcross.org

The American Red Cross, a humanitarian organization led by volunteers and guided by its congressional charter and the fundamental principles of the International Red Cross Movement, provides relief to victims of disasters and helps people prevent, prepare for, and respond to emergencies.

Asian Neighborhood Design
Maurice Lim Miller, Executive Director
461 Bush Street, Suite 400
San Francisco, CA 94108
415-982-2959

Asian Neighborhood Design (AND) is a nonprofit community development organization dedicated to advancing programs and policies that empower, transform, and improve the lives of low-income and disenfranchised individuals and communities in the Bay Area. AND's programs include: housing and community development; architecture and planning; family and youth resources; employment training to prepare participants for employment in woodworking, cabinetry, and related industries; and business development.

Barrios Unidos
Nane Alejandrez, Executive Director
1817 Soquel Avenue
Santa Cruz, CA 95062
831-457-8208

Barrios Unidos is a nonprofit community-based organization located in downtown Santa Cruz. Barrios Unidos strives to reduce violence among Latino youth. For nearly twenty years, Barrios Unidos has had a solid reputation for providing youth with the necessary education, support, and training to avoid and prevent violence in their lives.

Bidwell Training Center
Bill Strickland, President and CEO
1815 Metropolitan Street
Pittsburgh, PA 15233
412-323-4000

Established in 1968, Bidwell Training Center has attracted national recognition for its innovative and career-oriented training programs featuring strong partnerships with leading Pittsburgh corporations, agencies, and organizations. Bidwell is a nonprofit vocational/technical school that offers short-term accelerated programs geared toward equipping students with the necessary skills for employment in the high-tech, medical, culinary, and scientific fields.

Big Brothers Big Sisters of America
Judy Vredenburgh, President and CEO
230 North 13th Street
Philadelphia, PA 19107
215-567-7000
www.bbbsa.org

Big Brothers Big Sisters of America, the oldest mentoring organization serving youth in the country, has provided one-to-one mentoring relationships between adult volunteers and children at risk since 1904. BBBSA currently serves over 100,000 children and youth in more than 500 agencies throughout the United States.

Boys and Girls Clubs of America
Roxanne Spillet, President
1230 W. Peachtree Street NW
Atlanta, GA 30309
404-487-5700
www.bgca.org

The Boys and Girls Club movement is a nationwide affiliation of local, autonomous organizations and Boys and Girls Clubs of America working to help youth from all backgrounds, with special concern for those from disadvantaged circumstances, develop the qualities needed to become responsible citizens and leaders.

Building Opportunities for Self-Sufficiency (BOSS)
boona cheema, Executive Director
2065 Kittredge Street, Suite E
Berkeley, CA 94704
510-649-1930

For more than twenty-five years, Building Opportunities for Self-Sufficiency (BOSS, Inc., formerly known as Berkeley Oakland Support Services) has worked to elevate people out of poverty and home-lessness. BOSS provides a comprehensive array of housing services, employment programs, and opportunities to help individuals achieve self-sufficiency.

The Center for Homelessness
Drew Buscareno, Executive Director
813 South Michigan Street
South Bend, IN 46601
219-282-8700
www.center-for-homeless.com

The Center for Homelessness helps people break the cycle of home-lessness, operating a landscaping service in partnership with the ServiceMaster Corporation that employs homeless and formerly homeless persons. During its first season, CFH Landscape Services secured major contracts with local corporations, Memorial Hospital, the University of Notre Dame, and the City of South Bend.

The Chicago Children's Choir
Nancy Carstedt, Executive Director
Chicago Cultural Center
78 East Washington
Chicago, IL 60602
312-849-8300

The Chicago Children's Choir is a multiracial, multicultural children's choir dedicated to making a difference in young people's lives through musical excellence. The Chicago Children's Choir is America's largest, most comprehensive organization devoted to the musical edu-cation of children. Nearly 3,500 children participate in the Chicago Children's Choir programs.

Children's Health Fund
Irwin Redlener, President
317 East 64th Street
New York, NY 10021
212-535-9400
www.childrenshealthfund.org

The Children's Health Fund is committed to providing health care to the nation's most medically underserved children through the devel-opment and support of innovative primary care medical programs and the promotion of guaranteed access to appropriate health care for all children.

Children's Defense Fund
Marian Wright Edelman, President
25 E Street NW
Washington, DC 20001
202-628-8787
www.childrensdefense.org

"The mission of the Children's Defense Fund is to *Leave No Child Behind* and ensure every child a Healthy Start, a Head Start, a Fair Start, a Safe Start, and a Moral Start in life with a successful passage to adulthood through support of caring families and communities." Children's Defense Fund provides a strong, effective voice for all the children of America who cannot vote, lobby, or speak for themselves.

Chrysalis
Dave McDonough, Executive Director
516 South Main Street
Los Angeles, CA 90013
213-895-7777
www.chrysalisworks.org

Chrysalis helps people without homes and other economically disadvantaged individuals in greater Los Angeles become self-sufficient through employment opportunities. The guiding principle at Chrysalis is that a steady job is the single most important step in a person's transition to long-term self-sufficiency.

Citizen Schools
Eric Schwarz, President and Cofounder
308 Congress Street
Boston, MA 02210
617-695-2300
617-695-2367 (fax)

Citizen Schools is revolutionizing how children spend their out-of-school time—through fun, challenging, hands-on "apprenticeships" that unite volunteer citizen teachers and small groups of children, ages nine through fourteen. Children come away with practical skills they can use for life. Each apprenticeship also ends in a high-quality product or performance that allows children to be heroes in their own community. Founded in 1995 and now running at eleven Boston campuses, Citizen Schools serves twelve hundred students a year. Future plans include launching Citizen Schools University, with the aim of becoming a national innovator in the after-school field.

City Year
Alan Khazei, CEO
Michael Brown, President
285 Columbus Avenue
Boston, MA 02116
617-927-2500
www.cityyear.org

City Year taps the civic power of young people for an annual campaign of idealism. The goals of the annual campaign of idealism are to generate transformative service, break down social barriers, inspire citizens to civic action, develop new leaders for the common good, and improve and promote the concept of voluntary national service.

Common Ground Community
Rosanne Haggerty, Executive Director
14 East 28th Street
New York, NY 10016
212-471-0866
www.commonground.org

Common Ground Community is a not-for-profit corporation that develops innovative solutions to homelessness. Common Ground provides inventive, affordable housing that integrates comprehensive social and employment services and a supportive community to ensure that individuals remain stable and housed. Common Ground

Community owns and operates two Ben & Jerry's PartnerShops and the Top of the Times café, and earns further revenues from management of its property in New York.

Communities in Schools
Bill Milliken, President and Founder
277 South Washington Street, Suite 210
Alexandria, VA 22314
703-519-8999
www.cisnet.org

Founded in 1977, Communities in Schools (formerly known as Cities in Schools) is the nation's largest stay-in-school network, serving more than 300,000 young people through 121 local programs in 30 states. By relocating community service providers to work as personalized teams serving alongside teachers, principals, volunteers, and mentors, Communities in Schools connects the schools with the resources that students need most.

The Compass School
David Manzo, Executive Director
26 Sunnyside Street
Jamaica Plain, MA 02130
617-524-2333
www.compassinc.com

Compass is a private, nonprofit, community-based organization dedicated to serving inner-city children who have behavioral, social, and educational disabilities. The center offers comprehensive consulting services to public school systems and nonprofit organizations throughout the United States. Services include program evaluation, program development, liaison services with the Office of Civil Rights, and the planning and implementation of programs that seek to include students who have emotional and behavioral disabilities or who are at-risk in a general-education setting.

The Delancey Street Foundation
Dr. Mimi Silbert, President and CEO
600 Embarcadero
San Francisco, CA 94107
415-957-9800
www.citysearch7.com (search "delancey street")

The Delancey Street Foundation provides job training, peer counseling, shelter, food, and other necessities to people who want to overcome problems with crime, drugs, or alcohol. Delancey Street operates nine for-profit "training schools," which supply all the operating capital for the parent organization. These schools are located in five cities throughout the country and include a moving and trucking school, a restaurant and catering services school, a print and copy shop, retail and wholesale shops, and an automotive service center.

The Delta Foundation
Harry Bowie, President
819 Main Street
Greenville, MS 38701
662-335-5291

The Delta Foundation is a community development corporation dedicated to promoting economic, human, and social development of minority and economically underprivileged residents with the intent of eliminating poverty within the Mississippi Delta Region. The principal vehicle of the Delta Foundation's attack on poverty is the creation of for-profit enterprises that provide job opportunities for low-income people.

The Enterprise Foundation
Bart Harvey, CEO
American City Building
10227 Wincopin Circle, Suite 500
Columbia, MD 21044
410-964-1230
www.enterprisefoundation.org

The Enterprise Foundation is a national nonprofit housing and community-development organization that is dedicated to bringing lasting improvements to distressed communities. Enterprise and its related organizations have raised and leveraged $2.3 billion, and it has helped create more than 86,000 homes affordable to low-income Americans and place more than 30,000 people in jobs.

Esparanza Unida
Richard Oulahan, Executive Director
1329 West National
Milwaukee, WI 53204
414-671-0251

Esparanza Unida seeks to provide counseling, job training, and job placement services to minority, injured, and unemployed workers in the Milwaukee area. This twenty-four-year-old nonprofit community-development corporation operates seven training businesses including an auto repair and body shop, a housing rehabilitation business, a child-care center, a metal-fabrication shop, a catering business, and a used-car business.

First Book
Ms. Kyle Zimmer, Executive Director
1319 F Street NW, Suite 1000
Washington, DC 20004
202-393-1222
www.firstbook.org

First Book is a national nonprofit organization with a single mission: to give children from low-income families the opportunity to read and own their first new books. First Book works with existing literacy programs, effectively leveraging the efforts of local tutoring, mentoring, and family literacy organizations. In the year 2000, First Book distributed more than four million books to hundreds of thousands of children in more than 290 communities nationwide. First Book plans to expand and reach even more children and communities in the coming years.

Goodwill Industries International Office
George Kessinger, President and CEO
9200 Rockville Pike
Bethesda, MD 20814
301-530-6500
www.goodwill.org

Goodwill Industries is one of the world's largest nonprofit providers of employment and training services for people with disabilities and other disadvantaged conditions such as welfare dependency, illiteracy, criminal history, and homelessness.

The Greyston Foundation
Charles Lief, Executive Director
21 Park Avenue
Yonkers, NY 10703
914-376-3900

The Greyston Foundation provides strategic leadership, resource development, and management services to the Greyston operating companies, which include the Greyston Bakery, the Greyston Family Inn, the Greyston Child Care Center, Greyston Health Services, the Maitri Day Program, and the Greyston Garden Project.

Habitat for Humanity International
Millard Fuller, President
121 Habitat Street
Americus, GA 31709-3498
912-924-6935
www.habitat.org

Habitat for Humanity International is a nonprofit, ecumenical, Christian housing ministry dedicated to eliminating substandard housing and homelessness worldwide and to making adequate, affordable shelter a matter of conscience and action.

Heads Up

Vincent Pan, Executive Director
1101 Pennsylvania Avenue SE, Suite 100
Washington, DC 20003
202-544-4468
www.headsup-dc.org

Heads Up is a nonprofit organization that runs education and enrichment programs for children and families living in the most under-resourced parts of Washington, D.C. For its workforce, Heads Up draws particularly on the untapped potential of the city's college students, simultaneously helping these students understand their social responsibilities and training them in the leadership skills necessary to carry them out. Heads Up's efforts include daily after-school and summer programs for elementary school students, weekly college and job readiness activities for teenagers, ongoing support and training for parents, and a servant-leadership curriculum for college students.

Housing Works, Inc.

Charles King, President
594 Broadway, Suite 700
New York, NY 10012
212-966-0466
www.housingworks.org

Housing Works' mission is to help people living with AIDS and HIV who are homeless—or at risk of homelessness—to gain stability, security, and independence so that they can live their lives with hope and dignity. Housing Works operates three thrift shops in Manhattan, a used-book store/café, and an institutional food service and commercial catering business.

International Youth Foundation

Rick Little, President and CEO
32 South Street, Suite 500
Baltimore, MD 21202
410-347-1500
www.iyfnet.org

Founded in 1990, the International Youth Foundation (IYF) is dedicated to the positive development of children and youth, ages five to twenty, worldwide. IYF identifies effective programs and approaches that are making a profound and lasting difference in young lives and invests in them, strengthens their impact, and expands their reach so that many more young people may benefit.

Juma Ventures
Diane Flannery, CEO
10 United Nations Plaza, Suite 630
San Francisco, CA 94102
415-247-6580

Juma Ventures is a nonprofit organization that owns and operates small businesses in the Bay Area that provide training and employment opportunities for at-risk youth. Through its program, Workforce Resources, Juma Ventures helps young people from marginalized backgrounds develop the practical and emotional skills necessary to lead healthy and productive lives.

Manchester Craftsmen's Guild
Bill Strickland, Director
1815 Metropolitan Street
Pittsburgh, PA 15233
412-322-1773
www.manchesterguild.org

Manchester Craftsmen's Guild is a multidiscipline, minority-directed arts education organization in Pittsburgh that employs the visual arts and performing arts to: educate and inspire inner-city youth to become productive citizens; preserve, present, and promote jazz and visual arts to stimulate intercultural understanding, appreciation, and enhancement of the quality of life for their audiences; and equip and educate leaders to further demonstrate entrepreneurial potential.

Minnesota Diversified Industries, Inc.
Lloyd Bratland, President
1700 Wynne Avenue
St. Paul, MN 55108
651-646-2711

Minnesota Diversified Industries provides career opportunities for individuals with disabilities or disadvantages by creating economically viable
enterprises within an environment that is supportive of all employees.

National Trust for Historic Preservation
Richard Moe, President
1785 Massachusetts Avenue NW
Washington, DC 20036
202-588-6000
www.nationaltrust.org

The National Trust for Historic Preservation works to foster an appreciation of the diverse character and meaning of our American cultural
heritage and to preserve and revitalize the livability of our communities
by leading the nation in saving America's historical environments.

The Nature Conservancy
Steve Howell, COO
International Headquarters
4245 North Fairfax Drive, Suite 100
Arlington, VA 22203
703-841-5300
www.tnc.org

The Nature Conservancy preserves plants, animals, and natural communities that represent the diversity of life on Earth by protecting the
lands and waters that they need to survive.

New Community Corporation
Monsignor William J. Linder, Founder
233 West Market Street
Newark, NJ 07103
973-623-2800

New Community Corporation aims to help residents of inner cities improve the quality of their lives through a comprehensive approach that recognizes and meets the needs of the local community. In addition to helping with housing, human services, and individual development, New Community works to build a solid local economic base, provide jobs, and keep profits in the Newark community.

Pine Street Inn
Lyndia Downie, President
444 Harrison Avenue
Boston, MA 02118
617-482-4944
www.pinestreetinn.org

Pine Street Inn is committed to people in need of shelter, sustenance, and the basic moral and material supports necessary to lead a dignified and stable life. The mission of the inn, in all its programs, is to provide a community of respect and hope for each guest it serves, to be a resource through which neighbors and friends can help to meet the basic needs of others, and to serve as a national leader in the fight to end homelessness. Pine Street Inn operates a clothing warehouse and a thrift shop, and their culinary training program provides two thousand meals each day to emergency shelters and transitional guests.

Pioneer Human Services
Mike Burns, President
7440 West Marginal Way South
Seattle, WA 98108
206-768-1990

Pioneer Human Services provides rehabilitation, training, care, and employment to at-risk individuals in the Seattle area, including, but not limited to, alcohol- and drug-related cases, convicts, parolees, and persons on probation and under jurisdiction of the courts.

Reading Is Fundamental, Inc.
1825 Connecticut Avenue NW, Suite 400
Washington, DC 20009
877-RIF-READ (toll-free)
or 202-287-3220
www.rif.org

Reading Is Fundamental (RIF), Inc., develops and delivers children's and family literacy programs that help prepare young people for reading, and that motivate school-age children to read through a national grass-roots network of parents, teachers, librarians, and others. Many of the children RIF serves have economic or learning needs that put them at risk of failing to achieve basic educational goals. Today, thanks to public-private partnerships, RIF is the nation's largest children's and family literacy organization. By the end of 2001, RIF will have placed 200 million books in the hands and homes of America's children.

Rheedlen Centers
Geoffrey Canada, President and CEO
2770 Broadway
New York, NY 10025
212-866-0700
www.rheedlen.org

Founded in 1970, Rheedlen has developed a network of school-based prevention programs in Manhattan's Central Harlem, Upper West Side, and Hell's Kitchen neighborhoods that provides families and youth with a comprehensive array of services that keep young people in school while enhancing intellectual, social, and emotional development.

Rubicon Programs
Rick Aubry, Executive Director
2500 Bissell Avenue
Richmond, CA 94804
510-235-1516
www.rubiconpgms.org

Rubicon Programs provides a comprehensive and integrated continuum of social and rehabilitative services for individuals who face barriers preventing them from functioning independently and fully participating in the economic and social life of their communities. Rubicon operates in the Richmond area and runs an independent living program, a vocational training program, mental health services, and housing development. Rubicon also operates two businesses, Rubicon Buildings & Grounds and Rubicon Bakery.

Save the Children
Charles McCormick, President
54 Wilton Road
Westport, CT 06881
203-221-4000
www.savethechildren.org

Save the Children strives to make lasting, positive change in the lives of disadvantaged children. The organization works with families and communities in the United States and in over forty nations around the world, developing and managing integrated programs in health, education, economic opportunity, and emergency relief.

Second Harvest
Robert Forney, President
35 East Wacker Drive, Suite 2000
Chicago, IL 60601
312-263-2303
www.secondharvest.org

The largest charitable source of food in America, Second Harvest is a nationwide network of 185 food banks, supplying more than 40,000 local pantries, soup kitchens, homeless shelters, and other nonprofit agencies.

The SEED Foundation
Rajiv Vinnakota, Founder/President
Eric Adler, Founder/Executive Director
1010 16th Street NW, Suite 701
Washington, DC 20005
202-785-4123
www.seedfoundation.com

The mission of the SEED Foundation is to establish urban residential schools that prepare children, both academically and socially, for success in college and in the professional world. The foundation, created by individuals whose goal was to design and open schools to benefit inner-city children, established the first SEED school, the SEED Public Charter School of Washington, D.C., in 1998. As the school expands to a permanent campus in 2001 and full enrollment in 2004, it will serve as a model for additional targeted residential programs in the Washington, D.C., metropolitan area and elsewhere. Today the SEED Foundation provides ongoing organizational, fund-raising, and due diligence support for the school, including successful lobbying to provide additional funding for residential schools and major capital campaign management.

Share Our Strength
Bill Shore, Executive Director
733 15th Street NW, Suite 640
Washington, DC 20005
202-393-2925
www.strength.org
www.communitywealth.org

Share Our Strength (SOS) is one of the nation's leading antihunger, antipoverty organizations. By supporting food assistance, treating

malnutrition and other consequences of hunger, and promoting economic independence among people in need, SOS meets immediate
demands for food while investing in long-term solutions to hunger
and poverty. To meet its goals, SOS mobilizes industries and individuals to contribute their talents to fight hunger, and creates community wealth to promote lasting change.

Teach for America
Wendy Kopp, President
315 West 36th Street, 6th floor
New York, NY 10018
800-832-1230
www.teachforamerica.org

Teach for America sponsors the National Teacher Corps, talented,
dedicated, recent college graduates who commit two years to teach in
urban and rural public schools, which traditionally suffer from teacher
shortages. Since 1989, Teach for America has placed almost 5,000
teachers in thirteen geographic areas.

United Way of America
Chris Amundsen, President
701 N. Fairfax Street
Alexandria, VA 22314-2045
703-836-7100
www.unitedway.org

Through a vast network of volunteers and community service
agencies, United Way helps meet the health and human-care needs
of millions of people every day throughout America. The United
Way system includes approximately 1,400 community-based United Way
organizations. In total, voluntary contributions to United Way support approximately 45,000 agencies and chapters, helping millions of
people from all walks of life and income groups.

Venture Philanthropy Partners, Inc.
Mario Morino, Chairman
Gary Jonas, Managing Partner
11600 Sunrise Valley Drive, Suite 300
Reston, VA 20191
703-716-4050
www.venturephilanthropypartners.org

The goal of Venture Philanthropy Partners is to apply strategic investment management practices to build stronger, more effective, sustainable organizations serving children in the Washington, D.C., area.
Venture Philanthropy Partners will make its investments with two
purposes in mind: to have a significant impact on the organizations in
which it invests, and to learn how the venture philanthropy process
can work most effectively so that knowledge can be shared with others
nationally.

YMCA
Ken Gladish, Executive Director
101 N. Wacker Drive
Chicago, IL 60606
800-872-9622
www.ymca.net

Longtime leaders in community-based health, fitness, and aquatics,
YMCAs nationwide teach kids to swim, offer exercise classes for
people with disabilities, and lead adult aerobics. They also offer hundreds of other programs in response to community needs, including
camping, child care, teen clubs, environmental programs, substance
abuse prevention, youth sports, family nights, job training, and international exchange.

YWCA
Margaret Tyndall, Executive Director
350 Fifth Avenue, Suite 301
New York, NY 10118
212-273-7800
www.ywca.org

The YWCA is the largest and oldest women's membership movement in the United States. The mission of the YWCA is to empower women and girls and to eliminate racism. YWCAs offer shelter, child care, employment training, racial justice, physical fitness, youth development, and leadership training.

II. A sampling of national organizations that can help you find a way to give something back to your community through volunteerism includes:

America's Promise–The Alliance for Youth
Peter Gallagher, Executive Director
909 North Washington Street, Suite 400
Alexandria, VA 22314-1556
703-684-4500
www.americaspromise.org

America's Promise serves as a nationwide catalyst, urging public, private, and nonprofit organizations to focus their combined talents and resources to improve the lives of our nation's youth.

Corporation for National Service
1201 New York Avenue NW
Washington, DC 20525
202-606-5000
www.cns.gov

The Corporation for National Service works to engage Americans of all ages and backgrounds in community-based service that addresses the nation's education, public safety, and human and environmental needs to achieve direct and demonstrable results.

The Points of Light Foundation
Bob Goodwin, President and CEO
1400 I Street NW, Suite 800
Washington, DC 20005
202-729-8000
www.pointsoflight.org

Founded in May 1990, the Foundation is a nonpartisan, nonprofit organization devoted to promoting volunteerism. The Foundation is based in Washington, D.C., and supports communities throughout the United States through a network of over five hundred volunteer centers.

Youth Service America
Steve Culbertson, President and CEO
1101 15th Street, Suite 200
Washington, DC 20005
202-296-2992
www.servenet.org

Youth Service America is an alliance of organizations committed to community and national service. Youth Service America's mission is to build healthy towns and cities, and foster citizenship, knowledge, and personal development through a powerful network of service opportunities for young Americans.

III. A sampling of resourceful organizations for social entrepreneurs:

AddVenture Network
Richard Steckel, President
1350 Lawrence Street, Plaza 2H
Denver, CO 80204
303-572-3333

AddVenture Network offers consulting services to companies and individuals in six countries worldwide. AddVenture works with corporations wishing to be more socially responsible and profitable, and with social entrepreneurs in the nonprofit sector who are working to diversify their income while remaining true to their mission.

Ashoka: Innovators for the Public
Bill Drayton, President
1700 North Moore Street, Suite 2000
Arlington, VA 22209
703-527-8300
www.ashoka.org

Over a period of eighteen years, Ashoka has sought out and elected into its fellowship more than 900 fellows in Asia, Africa, Latin America, and, most recently, in Central Europe. At present, more than 100 new fellows are elected each year. Ashoka's investment in these social entrepreneurs yields regional and national advances in education, health, human rights, the environment, and other areas of social concern.

Community Wealth Ventures, Inc.
Bill Shore, Chairman
733 15th Street NW, Suite 6
Washington, DC 20005
202-393-1945
www.communitywealth.com

Community Wealth Ventures, a for-profit subsidiary of Share Our Strength, designs and builds community wealth—resources generated through profitable enterprise to promote social change—in order to maximize the impact of nonprofit organizations, corporations, and foundations working to strengthen America's communities.

The Conservation Company
John Riggan, CEO
One Penn Center, Suite 1550
Philadelphia, PA 19103
215-568-0399
www.consco.com

Formed in 1980, the Conservation Company is a multidisciplinary consulting firm with a team approach to working with nonprofit organizations, philanthropies, and corporate community involvement programs.

The Denali Initiative
William E. Strickland, Jr., President/CEO
Manchester/Bidwell Corporation
Donnie Day Pomeroy, Managing Director
Manchester Craftsmen Building
1815 Metropolitan Street
Pittsburgh, PA 15233
412-322-1773, ext. 204
www.denaliinitiative.org

The Denali Initiative is a leadership and social entrepreneurship development program for the executive directors of small to mid-size community-based not-for-profits. The Initiative is a three-year fellowship program grounded in the social-enterprise concept. Each participating organization comes to the program with a social-enterprise idea that is based on its mission; through the Initiative these organizations develop business and financial plans, raise startup funding, and research organizational readiness. The Denali Initiative is a unique collaboration between the Manchester Craftsmen's Guild and community, family, and national foundations.

The Peter F. Drucker Foundation for Nonprofit Management
Rob Johnston, President and CEO
320 Park Avenue, 3rd floor
New York, NY 10022
212-224-1174
www.pfdf.org

By providing educational opportunities and resources, The Peter F. Drucker Foundation furthers its mission to lead social-sector organizations toward excellence in performance. The Foundation pursues this mission through the presentation of conferences, video teleconferences, the annual Peter F. Drucker Award for Nonprofit Innovation, and the development of management resources, partnerships, and publications.

Echoing Green Foundation
198 Madison Avenue, 8th floor
New York, NY 10016
212-689-1165
www.echoinggreen.org

The Echoing Green Foundation offers fellowships to social entrepreneurs creating innovative public service organizations or projects that seek to catalyze positive social change.

The Kauffman Center for Entrepreneurial Leadership
Ewing Marion Kauffman Foundation
4801 Rockhill Road
Kansas City, MO 64110-2046
816-932-1000
www.emkf.org
www.entreworld.org

The Kauffman Center for Entrepreneurial Leadership at the Ewing Marion Kauffman Foundation was established in 1992 to stimulate entrepreneurial leadership in both the profit and nonprofit sectors; research, identify, teach, and disseminate the critical skills and values that enable entrepreneurs to succeed; introduce young people to the excitement and opportunity of entrepreneurship; and encourage others to support entrepreneurship.

The National Center for Social Entrepreneurs
Jim Thalhuber, President and CEO
5801 Duluth Street, Suite 310
Minneapolis, MN 55422
763-595-0890
www.socialentrepreneurs.org

The National Center for Social Entrepreneurs works to encourage entrepreneurship throughout the nonprofit sector and to help individual nonprofits create or expand social purpose business ventures.

The National Mentoring Partnership
Gail Manza, Executive Director
1600 Duke Street, Suite 300
Alexandria, VA 22314
703-224-2200
www.mentoring.org

The National Mentoring Partnership is an advocate for the expansion of mentoring and a resource for mentors and mentoring initiatives nationwide, forging partnerships at the national and local levels with community leaders and with schools, businesses, religious congregations, civic associations, and other institutions to help them make mentoring a reality for more children. The National Mentoring Partnership has helped more than 25,000 young people find mentors and has secured commitments from business and community leaders to recruit more than 300,000 new mentors for children throughout the country.

The Roberts Enterprise Development Fund
Jed Emerson, Founder
Melinda Tuan, Managing Director
Presidio Building 1009, first floor
P.O. Box 29266
San Francisco, CA 94129-0266
415-561-6677
www.redf.org

The Roberts Enterprise Development Fund portfolio consists of ten nonprofit organizations in the San Francisco Bay Area currently operating twenty-four enterprises providing transitional and permanent employment to very-low-income and formerly homeless individuals. The goal of the Fund is to assist these groups in achieving both increased scale and full sustainability in the marketplace.

Surdna Foundation
Ed Skloot, Executive Director
330 Madison Avenue, 30th floor
New York, NY 10017-5001
212-557-0003
www.surdna.org

The Surdna Foundation is interested in fostering catalytic, entrepreneurial programs that offer viable solutions to difficult systemic problems. They also seek high quality, direct service programs that advance the foundation's philanthropic goals. Surdna makes grants in the following program areas: environment, community revitalization, effective citizenry, the arts, nonprofit sector support, and organizational capacity-building grants.

Acknowledgments

The word "acknowledgment" does not begin to convey my gratitude for the friends, family, and camerado who shared or indulged the conviction that this book is important.

The staffs and boards of directors of Share Our Strength and Community Wealth Ventures supported the writing with research, ideas, and revisions. They filled in for me during my absences. Their day-in, day-out dedication to giving both support and dignity to the people we serve is a constant source of inspiration. There are too many to name, but a few whose long tenures deserve special note include Hadley Boyd, Kelly Carey, Jody Franklin, Ashley Graham, and Jeanne Robinson. Also, Cathy Townsend, who every day reignites the Share Our Strength spirit, Sondra Friedman, who ensures that our message reaches a broader audience, and Pat Nicklin, who so ably leads our executive team. As she has always been, my sister Debbie Shore is in a category all her own. Candid adviser, defender, protector, and friend, Debbie has shown a commitment that uniquely transcends Share Our Strength. It has endured for a lifetime.

Just as these pages could not cohere without binder's glue, my own work would not hold together, be organized, or make sense without the glue that is Chuck Scofield, my executive assistant. Chuck's peripheral vision, research and writing talent, organized memory, friendship, and encouragement were invaluable. No one did more to make this book better.

The most precious gifts a writer can enjoy are time and a place to write. I received such gifts from Brian Frawley, Augustinian College, Jean-Jacques and Maries Raoul, and Diane and Jerry Stubbs. I received those gifts and more from Zach and Mollie Shore, and also Bonnie Shore, who was as unselfish in support of this book as she is in everything else she does.

Carter Echols at Washington National Cathedral made available to me that national treasure, which was a rich source of material, inspiration, and great personal joy.

I'm grateful to those who allowed the intrusion of my looking at their work from many angles: Nancy Carstedt, Noel Cunningham, Alan Khazei, Michael Brown, Geoffrey Canada, and Gary Mulhair and Mara Manus, who have continued and expanded their efforts at the national level, Gary now at Community Wealth Ventures, and Mara now at the Ford Foundation.

Special thanks to the pros. My editor, Jon Karp, did what the best editors do, steering me gently past my blind spots and away from unfinished thoughts, toward ideas that could make a difference. His confidence was contagious, and his patience comforting. I will long be grateful for his commitment to this book. Flip Brophy is my agent, advocate, and dear friend. If books didn't exist, I would invent them just to work with her each day. Thanks also to Ann Godoff, president of Random House, for wanting this book to count.

I'd also like to thank those friends who have gone out of their way and beyond the scope of generosity to support our work. They include: Ken Adelsberg, Kathy Bushkin, Ray Chambers, Ed Cohen, Joni Doolin, Wally Doolin, Joel Fleishman, David Gardner, Tom Gardner, George Gendron, Gary Hirshberg, David House, Ira Jackson, Dean Kasperzak, Dan Maffey, Alan Meltzer, Mario Morino, General Colin Powell, Mark Rodriguez, Jon Rubin, Eli Segal, Arman Simone, Ed Skloot, Jeff Swartz, Tom Tolworthy, Mark Warner, and Lloyd Wirshba. Each and every one has shared their strength.

About the Author

BILL SHORE is the founder and executive director of Share Our Strength, a national nonprofit organization that has raised more than $150 million to support antihunger and antipoverty organizations worldwide since its founding in 1984 and has mobilized tens of thousands of individuals to contribute their talents to its efforts. Shore is also chairman of Community Wealth Ventures, Inc., a subsidiary of Share Our Strength, which provides strategic counsel to corporations, foundations, and nonprofit organizations interested in creating community wealth. He is the author of *Revolution of the Heart* and *The Light of Conscience*. He lives outside Washington, D.C., and can be reached via e-mail at bshore@strength.org.

About the Type

This book was set in Perpetua, a typeface designed by the English artist Eric Gill, and cut by the Monotype Corporation between 1928 and 1930. Perpetua is a contemporary face of original design, without any direct historical antecedents. The shapes of the roman letters are derived from the techniques of stonecutting. The larger display sizes are extremely elegant and form a most distinguished series of inscriptional letters.